THE HORSE RACING MISCELLANY

JOHN WHITE

WITH A FOREWORD BY LESTER PIGGOTT

CARLTON
BOOKS

ACKNOWLEDGEMENTS

I would like to say a special word of thanks to Lester Piggott for so very kindly agreeing to write the foreword to my book. It is such a privilege to have the greatest jockey the world has ever seen, a true king of "the sport of kings", associated with my book.

LeeAnn at www.famousracehorses.co.uk was kind enough to read my work in order to ensure that the entries are as accurate as possible.

I would also like to thank my wife, Janice, and my two sons, Marc and Paul, for all of their support in helping me compile my book.

THE HORSE RACING MISCELLANY

This book is dedicated to two very special men, both of whom I regret to say are no longer with us – my father, John McDermot White, and my father-in-law, Bobby McWilliams.

We miss you both so very much but know that there is not a single day that goes by when you are far from our thoughts, safe in the knowledge that you are watching over your families.

I would also like to mention my nephews and nieces: Aisling, Amy-Jo, Claire, David, Fiona, John-Preston, Niamh, Paris, Paul, Ryan, Shasta-Naomi and Shea.

John

This edition published in 2009

Carlton Books Limited
20 Mortimer Street
London W1T 3JW

A CIP catalogue record for this book is available from the British Library

ISBN: 978-1-84732-315-6

Editor: Martin Corteel
Project Art Editor: Paul Chattaway
Production: Luca Bazzoli

Printed in Great Britain

FOREWORD

I was pleased to accept when John asked me to write this foreword to his *Horse Racing Miscellany.* My thanks to Carlton Publishing for making a most generous donation to The Injured Jockeys Fund and the Sir Peter O'Sullevan Trust.

As the son and grandson of trainers who were previously jockeys – mainly over jumps – I grew up in a racing environment and ever since I can remember I took it for granted that I would be a jockey. In 1948, aged 12, I rode my first winner, The Chase, at Haydock. She was trained by my father. That set the scene for the next 50 years, until, at Haydock Park again, I signed off on Palacegate Jack, trained by Jack Berry.

Being a jockey is a hectic life, particularly with the introduction of evening and Sunday fixtures, making it a non-stop, year round "racing season". Riding gallops for your principal trainer early in the morning, then a 2–4 hour journey to the track with up to 10 rides in a day – if there was evening racing – and back home by midnight became commonplace. Sundays usually took in riding on the continent, mainly in France, Italy, Germany and Spain, and winters were spent visiting racecourses around the world – the USA, Canada, the Caribbean and South America, South Africa, Rhodesia (as it was then), Mauritius, India, the Middle and Far East and Australasia.

During my career I have been lucky enough to work with some truly great horses and some of the world's best trainers. However, whether you are a jockey, trainer, breeder or owner, all of which I have been, you are nothing without a dedicated and loyal team of stable staff, and to them I would like to pay the highest tribute.

Thoroughbred horse racing has long been dubbed "the sport of kings". Today, it is true, you are more likely to find a prince, a princess, sheikh or sultan at the racecourse rather than a king, but let us not forget that Her Majesty still enjoys plenty of success. However, horse racing is also the sport of those who just like a flutter on the Grand National or a trip to Ladies' Day at Ascot once a year. It is a sport that continues to thrill and excite, and this book, with its statistics, anecdotes, quirky facts and tributes to the great and the good, will enthral any enthusiast.

Lester Piggott
December 2008

NOTES

References to the Derby and the Oaks are always the races at Epsom unless otherwise indicated, i.e. the Irish Derby and Oaks (at The Curragh), the French Derby (or Prix du Jockey Club – Prix de Diane for fillies – at Chantilly) and Kentucky Derby (at Churchill Downs, Kentucky).

Horse racing in Britain refers only to the 60 courses in England, Scotland and Wales. Down Royal and Downpatrick are both in Northern Ireland but they come under the auspices of Horse Racing Ireland. Ireland has 27 courses, of which 23 are dual purpose and only one, Kilbeggan, is jumps only (the beach track at Laytown, The Curragh and Dundalk stage only flat meetings).

Race distances in Britain are in miles and furlongs. A furlong is 220 yards (approximately 200 metres) and there are eight furlongs to a mile. The Derby is run over 1½ miles or 2,400 metres. The weights horses carry are measured in stones and pounds. A pound (lb) is approximately 0.453kg and a stone (st) – 14lbs – around 6.35kg.

Winning margins are measured in lengths. These used to be the length of a horse, but they are now measured in time. In flat races, one length is 0.2 seconds; in National Hunt a length is 0.25 seconds. In ascending order distances between horses can be: a nose, a short-head, a head, a neck, ¼ length, ½ length ¾ length, length, and so on, up to around 25 lengths, after which "distance" is used.

The colour of a horse may be black or brown, which are self-explanatory, bay (a lighter shade of brown), chestnut (auburn to ginger) or grey (from dark silver to white). Very occasionally there are horses which are piebald (black and white irregular patches) or roan (brown and white). The difference between a grey and a roan is that a grey will become lighter or whiter in colour as it ages.

INTRODUCTION

Since the inaugural English Classic, the St Leger in 1776, I have no doubt many barons, earls, lords, marquesses and the odd king or two have all, at one time, been willing to make a pact with the dark side to grant him that elusive thoroughbred that would see his name enshrined in the long and illustrious history of horse racing in return for all his earthly possessions. There can be few better moments in sport than owning, training or riding the winner of the coveted Derby at Epsom or the Grand National at Aintree.

However, despite being labelled "the sport of kings", the world of thoroughbred horse racing offers a long, hard road to success for the jockeys who practically starve their bodies of all those enjoyable things that we normal human beings take for granted, the trainers who assume overall responsibility for the success or failure of a colt or filly regardless of progeny, and the owners who can spend their entire wealth on landing that most coveted of prizes, a champion thoroughbred. But what memorable moments these three key ingredients to horse racing immortality have given us over the years, none more so than the legendary Nijinsky's Triple Crown success in 1970 with the immortal Lester Piggott at his controls.

From an early age I was introduced to this intriguing, yet captivating sport, not from a saddle, nor from grooming and certainly not through ownership, but through betting. My father, John McDermot White, loved nothing better than a flutter on the "gee-gees". It used to drive my mum to distraction, cue the millions of others who can empathize with her, but as my mum always said it was Dad's only "vice" because he did not smoke or drink. I must have been the only kid growing up in the Short Strand, Belfast, during the 1970s who did not have to go to the local pub to tell his dad his tea was on the table. Instead, I would retrieve him from the bookie's clutches.

Dad's favourite was Lester Piggott, and although I was more into football and Georgie Best, I could see why my dad had such a fascination with "The Long Fellow". Whereas some women are jealous of their husband's lovers or cars, I have no doubt that my mum was envious of this 5-foot, 7½-inch tall man, who weighed just 8 stone, wore long black leather boots and was dressed from head to foot in rich silks. And you can bet all the money you have in the world, that if there is horse racing in heaven, my dad will be at every meeting with a docket in one hand, and as Mum would say a "beaten one"!

John White
December 2008

ONE TIME ONLY

A horse can only win the 1000 Guineas, 2000 Guineas, the Oaks and the Derby once each as they are strictly races for three-year-olds.

A TRUE CHAMPION

In 1979 jockey Bob Champion was diagnosed as having testicular cancer. Champion was given eight months to live with only a 40 per cent chance of survival by the doctors, but he vowed to fight it and commenced a very aggressive programme of chemotherapy. During this time he often said that the only thing that kept him going was that he hoped one day to ride Aldaniti in the Grand National.

Champion returned to racing within a year but the chemotherapy had taken its toll on his body leaving him with an infection that almost killed him. So he postponed his dream of partnering Aldaniti in the 1980 race. The following year his dream came true when he and Aldaniti, trained by Josh Gifford, landed the National. Champion and Aldaniti's achievement won the pair the BBC Sports Personality Team of the Year award in 1981. Champion's heroics were immortalized in the movie *Champions*, while a bar was named after Aldiniti at Aintree. The Aldaniti Bar is beneath the Lord Sefton Stand, which is located after the winning post at the bend that sees the horses going out for the start of the second circuit.

Champion was awarded an MBE in 1983 and that same year he formed the Bob Champion Cancer Trust, which has raised millions of pounds for cancer research.

COMMONLY KNOWN AS

The Oaks is referred to as "The Fillies' Derby".

RACING SCANDALS (1)

In 1844, Running Rein won the Derby but was subsequently disqualified when Lord George Bentinck discovered that he was in fact a four-year-old named Maccabeus (he ran in the race under three-year-old Running Rein's name). The race was awarded to the second-placed horse Orlando (ridden by Nat Flatman) whose owner, Colonel Jonathan Peel, successfully sued. It was a bad year for the Derby when it was also discovered that one of the runners was a six-year-old and the second favourite for the race was tampered with the night before and pulled up by his jockey.

FROM THE HORSE'S MOUTH (1)

"A roistering party at a country house founded two races and named them gratefully after their host and his house, the Derby and the Oaks. Seldom has a carouse had more permanent affect."
The 5th Earl of Rosebery *(1847–1929), owner of three Derby winners, Ladas in 1894, Sir Visto in 1895 and Cicero in 1905.*

THE 1000 GUINEAS

The 1000 Guineas is one of the five English Classics, a Group 1 race for three-year-old thoroughbred fillies only. It is run over a distance of 1 mile on the famous Rowley Mile course at Newmarket in late April or early May. The inaugural 1000 Guineas took place on 28 April 1814, five years after the inaugural 2000 Guineas. the first winner was Charlotte, ridden by Bill Clift, trained by Tom Perren and owned by Christopher Wilson. Charlotte's owner received the sum of 1,000 guineas (a guinea was £1 and 1 shilling – or £1.05 in modern currency), the Classic's original winning purse.

WHEN THE TOUGH GET GOING

The world's oldest Classic, the St Leger has one of the longest and most demanding home straights in the world of racing. The 4½ gruelling furlongs of the Doncaster course can see a horse go from first to halfway down the field in seconds as the turf saps the strength of even the fittest entry.

RACING JARGON (1)

Allowance – this is the term given to varying amounts of weight that are taken off the published weights carried by horses in a race. In certain types of races, horses are allocated less weight because they are younger, and fillies/mares also carry less weight than colts/geldings. There are also allowances, or claims, for jockeys, normally the youngest and least experienced – called apprentices on the flat and conditionals in National Hunt. The allowances are normally three, five or seven pounds, though in races exclusively for apprentices/conditionals an extra pound is given if the jockey rides a horse trained by his employer. On a racecard, a jockey's allowance in pounds is in brackets after his name. Until recently there was an age limit for jockeys to claim an allowance, but it drops as they win more races, and, in Britain, is removed when they have ridden 95 winners.

ST LEGER WINNERS 1946–2008

Year	*Winner*	*Jockey*	*Trainer*
2008	Conduit	Frankie Dettori	Sir Michael Stoute
2007	Lucarno	Jimmy Fortune	John Gosden
2006**	Sixties Icon	Frankie Dettori	Jeremy Noseda
2005	Scorpion	Frankie Dettori	Aidan O'Brien
2004	Rule of Law	Kerrin McEvoy	Saeed bin Suroor
2003	Brian Boru	Jamie Spencer	Aidan O'Brien
2002	Bollin Eric	Kevin Darley	Tim Easterby
2001	Milan	Michael Kinane	Aidan O'Brien
2000	Millenary	Richard Quinn	John Dunlop
1999	Mutafaweq	Richard Hills	Saeed bin Suroor
1998	Nedawi	John Reid	Saeed bin Suroor
1997	Silver Patriarch	Pat Eddery	John Dunlop
1996	Shantou	Frankie Dettori	John Gosden
1995	Classic Cliche	Frankie Dettori	Saeed bin Suroor
1994	Moonax	Pat Eddery	Barry Hills
1993	Bob's Return	Philip Robinson	Mark Tompkins
1992	User Friendly	George Duffield	Clive Brittain
1991	Toulon	Pat Eddery	André Fabre
1990	Snurge	Richard Quinn	Paul Cole
1989*	Michelozzo	Steve Cauthen	Henry Cecil
1988	Minster Son	Willie Carson	Neil Graham
1987	Reference Point	Steve Cauthen	Henry Cecil
1986	Moon Madness	Pat Eddery	John Dunlop
1985	Oh So Sharp	Steve Cauthen	Henry Cecil
1984	Commanche Run	Lester Piggott	Luca Cumani
1983	Sun Princess	Willie Carson	Dick Hern
1982	Touching Wood	Paul Cook	Harry Thomson Jones
1981	Cut Above	Joe Mercer	Dick Hern
1980	Light Cavalry	Joe Mercer	Henry Cecil
1979	Son of Love	Alain Lequeux	Robert Collet
1978	Julio Mariner	Eddie Hide	Clive Brittain
1977	Dunfermline	Willie Carson	Dick Hern
1976	Crow	Yves Saint-Martin	Angel Penna Sr
1975	Bruni	Tony Murray	Ryan Price
1974	Bustino	Joe Mercer	Dick Hern
1973	Peleid	Frankie Durr	Bill Elsey
1972	Boucher	Lester Piggott	Vincent O'Brien
1971	Athens Wood	Lester Piggott	Harry Thomson Jones
1970	Nijinsky	Lester Piggott	Vincent O'Brien
1969	Intermezzo	Ron Hutchinson	Harry Wragg

Year	Winner	Jockey	Trainer
1968	Ribero	Lester Piggott	F. Johnson Houghton
1967	Ribocco	Lester Piggott	F. Johnson Houghton
1966	Sodium	Frankie Durr	George Todd
1965	Provoke	Joe Mercer	Dick Hern
1964	Indiana	Jimmy Lindley	Jack Watts
1963	Ragusa	Garnie Bougoure	Paddy Prendergast
1962	Hethersett	Harry Carr	Dick Hern
1961	Aurelius	Lester Piggott	Noel Murless
1960	St Paddy	Lester Piggott	Noel Murless
1959	Cantelo	Eddie Hide	Charles Elsey
1958	Alcide	Harry Carr	Cecil Boyd-Rochfort
1957	Ballymoss	Tommy Burns	Vincent O'Brien
1956	Cambremer	Freddie Palmer	Georges Bridgland
1955	Meld	Harry Carr	Cecil Boyd-Rochfort
1954	Never Say Die	Charlie Smirke	Joe Lawson
1953	Premonition	Eph Smith	Cecil Boyd-Rochfort
1952	Tulyar	Charlie Smirke	Marcus Marsh
1951	Talma	Rae Johnstone	Charles Semblat
1950	Scratch	Rae Johnstone	Charles Semblat
1949	Ridge Wood	Michael Beary	Noel Murless
1948	Black Tarquin	Edgar Britt	Cecil Boyd-Rochfort
1947	Sayajirao	Edgar Britt	Sam Armstrong
1946	Airborne	Tommy Lowrey	Dick Perryman

** The 1989 race was run at Ayr after being postponed at Doncaster a week earlier.*

*** The 2006 race was run at York over the slightly shorter distance of 1 mile 5 furlongs 197 yards.*

I THOUGHT I WON THE DERBY!

Shergar so completely dominated the 1981 Derby, pulling clear after 3 furlongs to eventually win the Classic by a record 10 lengths, that John Matthias on the runner-up Glint of Gold thought he had won. "I told myself I'd achieved my life's ambition. Only then did I discover there was another horse on the horizon," said a bedazzled Matthias.

SHERGAR IN DISGUISE

The computer game *Rome: Total War: Barbarian Invasion* makes a reference to a Hunnic horsegod named Ragrehs, which is "Shergar" spelt backwards in tribute to the legendary winner of the 1981 Derby.

FRED ARCHER

There can have been few more tragic tales than that of Fred Archer, the greatest jockey of the 19th century and maybe of all time. Frederick James Archer was born in Cheltenham on 11 January 1857 into a horse racing family. His father William rode the winner of the 1858 Grand National and, at the age of 11, Fred was apprenticed to top trainer Matthew Dawson at Newmarket. In September 1870, at Chesterfield, Athol Daisy gave Archer his first victory under rules.

The first clouds on Archer's horizon soon appeared as he continued to grow, eventually reaching 5ft 10in, very tall for a flat jockey, and with that came the problems of weight. In 1874, 17-year-old Archer had already lost his apprentice claims, but Dawson made him his stable jockey and, in that year, Archer rode the Dawson-trained Atlantic to victory in the 2000 Guineas, his first Classic. Archer ended 1874 as Champion Jockey. There would be no other during his lifetime.

The era's leading owner and breeder, Lord Falmouth, was quick to appoint him as his retained jockey and the pair, with Dawson, formed a dominant partnership, with Silvio providing Derby glory in 1877. Archer rode four more Derby winners, but only one – Melton in 1885 – with Dawson. His other three Derby successes came on Bend Or in 1880, Iroquois (1881) and Ormonde (1886), while he won four Oaks, two 1000 Guineas, four 2000 Guineas, six St Legers, plus the French Derby twice and the Grand Prix de Paris three times.

Although he was the ultimate big race jockey, Archer gave his best whether riding in a Classic or a claimer. The winners came regularly and his success rate of 2,748 winners from 8,084 rides is better than a victory in every three races. He was the first jockey to ride 200 winners in a season and he did so eight times.

Archer married Helen Rose Dawson, a niece of the trainer, in January 1883, but it was a tragically short-lived marriage. Their first child, a boy, died just a few days after his birth, and Helen didn't survive the birth of their second child, a girl, in November 1884. Although Archer won 13 consecutive jockeys' titles – including a record 246 winners in 1885, a mark which stood for 48 years – life was a struggle, especially with his weight problems. A gambling addiction – jockeys could gamble in those days – and a bout of typhoid added to his burdens. On 8 November 1886, aged just 29, Archer shot himself at Newmarket.

Did You Know That?

Archer was Champion Jockey in 1880 despite missing two months with a a serious arm injury and had piloted Bend Or to Derby glory with one arm held together by an iron splint.

RUMMY'S IMPRESSIVE NUMBERS

In total Red Rum ran at Aintree seven times, winning four (the 1967 Thursby Selling Plate in which he dead-heated with Curlicue and his three National wins) and coming second in the other three. During Rummy's 10-year racing career he had 24 different jockeys, including Lester Piggott, five different trainers, won three flat races and raced 100 times over jumps, winning three hurdle races and 21 steeplechases. He was also placed 55 times (10 of these in flat races) and landed both the Scottish Grand National (1974) and the Grand National Trial at Haydock Park.

2000 GUINEAS

The race is for three-year-old thoroughbred colts and fillies and is usually a good guide to the form of a potential Derby winner. It is run over a distance of 1 mile at Newmarket Racecourse annually in late April or early May on the Saturday of the Guineas meeting. The race derives its name from the original guaranteed prize fund made available to the winner of the inaugural running of the race in 1809. The race is run over the famous Rowley Mile course, named after King Charles II (nicknamed "Old Rowley"), who founded the Newmarket meetings in the 17th century.

RACING JARGON (2)

Hands – the unit of measurement for calculating the height of a horse from the withers (top of the shoulder blades) to the ground. One hand is equivalent to 10 centimetres (4 inches). Most racehorses stand approximately 16 hands high.

HUNT CUP OVERSHADOWS GOLD CUP

Until the late 1930s the most prestigious race of the Cheltenham Festival was the 4-mile National Hunt Cup, with the horses all maidens and ridden by amateur jockeys. This is borne out by the prize money offered for the respective winning purses of the National Hunt Cup and the Cheltenham Gold Cup. In 1936 Pucka Belle collected £1,155 after winning the Hunt Cup and the legendary Golden Miller picked up a meagre £670 for winning his fifth consecutive Gold Cup. After the Second World War the Hunt Cup began to lose its importance on the National Hunt calendar and was surpassed by both the Gold Cup and the Champion Hurdle.

ARKLE

Arkle was, unquestionably, one of the greatest horses of the 20th century and the greatest steeplechaser of all time. He was foaled on 19 April 1957, sired by Archive out of Bright Cherry. His grandsire was Nearco. Arkle was bred at Ballymacoll Stud, County Meath, Ireland, by Mrs Mary Alison Baker and was owned by Anne Grosvenor, the Duchess of Westminster. He was trained by Tom Dreaper at Greenogue, Kilsallaghan, County Dublin, and, throughout his chasing career, ridden by Pat Taaffe.

His first win came in January 1962 at Navan in a novice hurdle, romping home at the generous odds of 20-1, ahead of his stablemate Kerforo, a future Irish Grand National winner. Following two more victories over hurdles Arkle travelled to England for the first time. In November 1962 he raced at Cheltenham and won by a staggering 20 lengths. The racing world knew there and then that he was a special horse. The following March Arkle returned to Cheltenham and dominated the Broadway Chase (now the Royal & Sun Alliance).

In late 1963 Arkle finished third to Mill House in the Hennessy Cognac Gold Cup at Newbury after slipping on landing at the fourth last. Four months later he faced Mill House in the Cheltenham Gold Cup, with the latter the odds-on favourite. However, Arkle and Taaffe had other ideas and won the race by five lengths. Arkle went off at 7-4 second favourite, the last time he would not start a race as the jolly. Next time out, in the Irish Grand National, Arkle was burdened with 2½ stone more to carry than his rivals but he was still too good for the field, winning by a length.

The following season's Hennessy Gold Cup saw Arkle at his majestic best defeating Mill House by 20 lengths at odds of 3-10. He retained the Cheltenham Gold Cup in 1965 and in 1966 started the race as the 1-10 favourite to land his third consecutive Cheltenham Gold Cup. Arkle destroyed the field, winning the race by 30 lengths. He ended the 1965–66 season unbeaten in his five starts, with many owners refusing to test their horses against Arkle, such was his dominance. Arkle also won three consecutive Leopardstown Chases in his Gold Cup-winning years (1964–66). Sadly, he was injured in the 1966 King George VI Chase at Kempton Park and never ran again.

Arkle won 27 of his 35 starts, earning £95,200 in prize money, at distances from 1mile, 6 furlongs to 3 miles, 5 furlongs.

Did You Know That?
The Irish National Stud at Tully, County Kildare, has the skeleton of Arkle on display in its museum.

NASHWAN'S GLORY DAY AT EPSOM

The 1989 Derby was won by the pre-race favourite Nashwan, ridden by Willie Carson and trained by Major Dick Hern. His winning time was 2 minutes, 34.90 seconds. Prior to his Derby success Nashwan won the 2000 Guineas and after winning at Epsom he also landed that year's Eclipse Stakes and the King George VI and Queen Elizabeth Diamond Stakes, the first and to date only horse to land this unique quadruple. He was the first horse to complete the Guineas–Derby Double since Nijinsky in 1970. Nashwan's progeny includes Swain (foaled in 1992), who won the King George VI and Queen Elizabeth Diamond Stakes twice (1997 and 1998) and Bago (foaled in 2001), who won the Prix de l'Arc de Triomphe in 2004. He ran seven times, always ridden by Willie Carson, and won six times, earning £793,248 in prize money. His only defeat was in the 1989 Prix Niel at Longchamp. Nashwan, who died on 19 July 2002 at Shadwell Stud, Newmarket, was given a Timeform rating of 135.

Did You Know That?
Bitmap Brothers, a British-based computer game developer, have included references to Nashwan in several of their games including *Speedball 2*.

THE AMERICANS OCCUPY AINTREE

The Grand National was not run between 1941 and 1945. During this time more thean 16,000 American troops were stationed at Aintree and the Stars and Stripes was hung from the flagstaff.

THE FILLIES TRIPLE CROWN

The British Fillies Triple Crown comprises the 1000 Guineas, the Oaks and the St Leger. Only seven horses have won the coveted title, the last being Oh So Sharp in 1985.

THE RACE OF CHAMPIONS

In 1991 the Jenny Pitman-trained Garrison Savannah, ridden by her son, Mark, won the Cheltenham Gold Cup. This Gold Cup had probably the strongest ever field for the race as it included not only the 1989 winner (Desert Orchid) and the defending champion (Norton's Coin) but also two future winners in Cool Ground (1992) and The Fellow (1994).

PRINCE CHARLES DELAYS THE NATIONAL

The start time of the 2005 Grand National at Aintree was moved back by 25 minutes as a result of the wedding of Prince Charles and Camilla Parker Bowles.

FIVE-YEAR-OLD CHAMPION

On 11 March 2008, the Irish bred Katchit, trained by Alan King and ridden by Robert "Chocolate" Thornton, became the first five-year-old to win the Champion Hurdle at Cheltenham since See You Then claimed victory in 1985. See You Then also won the race in 1986 and 1987.

FROM THE HORSE'S MOUTH (2)

"In terms of raw ability, Nijinsky was probably the best. He got nervous before his races, and I was always anxious until he had jumped out of the stalls. Then he'd drop the bit and you could put him anywhere in a race. Soon after the King George he got ringworm, and ran in the St Leger, probably before he'd really got over it. It was the Triple Crown and no horse had landed it since Bahram in 1935, so you can understand why they wanted him to go. He won all right, but not as easily as people thought."
***Lester Piggott** during an interview with* The Observer *on 6 May 2001*

STEADY ON HIS FEET

Red Rum never actually fell in a race although he once unseated his rider and once slipped up (both times at Haydock Park).

IRISH ST LEGER

The Irish St Leger is a Group 1 flat horse race that is run in September at The Curragh, County Kildare. The Irish Classic is open to three-year-old thoroughbred colts and is run over a distance of 1 mile, 6 furlongs. The inaugural Irish St Leger was run in 1915 when it was contested by three-year-old fillies only and was won by La Poloma. The race has been sponsored by The *Irish Field* newspaper since 2003 and there is currently a bonus prize of Aus$500,000 offered to any winner who subsequently wins the Melbourne Cup in the same year.

THE A–Z OF BETTING SLANG

Asian handicap: No dead heats in a race.
Banker: The horse most consider will win the race.
Burlington Bertie: Odds of 100 to 30.
Carpet (or gimmel): Odds of 3 to 1. Double carpet is 33 to 1.
Dime bet: US betting slang for a $1,000 stake.
Full cover: Multiple bet covering all possible permutations.
Goliath: Multiple bet comprising 247 individual bets from 8 selections in 8 different betting events, it consists of 28 doubles, 56 trebles, 70 quads, 56 five-ways, 28 six-ways, 8 seven-ways and one accumulator of all eight.
Heinz: Multiple bet comprising 57 different bets from 6 different selections, consisting of 15 doubles, 20 trebles, 15 quads, 6 five-ways and one accumulator of all six.
Jolly: The favourite in a race.
Kite: A cheque.
Lay: When the bookie accepts a bet from a punter.
Monkey: A £500 bet.
Nap: A term used by tipsters to identify their most confident selection of the day and/or card.
Pony: A £25 bet.
Punter: Someone who places a bet.
Return: Winnings.
Scalper: A punter who plays one bookie off against another by betting on both competitors in an event at odds that will mean he will earn a profit regardless of who actually wins.
Tipster: A person who gives tips.
Union Jack: Multiple bet of 8 trebles from 9 selections; on a betting slip, it looks like a Union Jack flag.
Value bet: The most generous odds for a particular bet.
Yankee: Multiple bet comprising 11 bets from 4 selections, 6 doubles, 4 trebles and 1 quad.

1000 GUINEAS COPYCATS

The format of the 1000 Guineas has been adopted by many racing authorities around the world, giving birth to such races as the French Jockey Club's Poule d'Essai des Pouliches, the Irish 1000 Guineas, the German 1000 Guineas and Italy's Premio Regina.

INDIAN OATH

Oath, winner of the 1999 Derby with Kieren Fallon aboard, became the first and to date only Derby winner to be placed at stud in India. Following his Derby success Oath looked all set to add the King George VI and Queen Elizabeth Diamond Stakes to his CV only to break down during the race. This resulted in his owner, Mr Fahd Salman, selling him for stud duties in Japan. Things did not go to plan in Japan and Oath was packed off to Ireland, where he was entered in a sale in 2006 and purchased by Mr Rajendra Singh Idar for his Pratap Stud Farm at Himmatnagar, India.

SCOTTISH NATIONAL TREBLE

In the history of the Scottish Grand National (1867–2008) only three horses have won the race three times: Couvrefeu II (1911, 1912 and 1913), Southern Hero (1934, 1936 and 1939) and Queen's Taste (1953, 1954 and 1956).

RACING JARGON (3)

Dam: The mother of a horse
Sire: The father of a horse
Grand sire: The grandfather of a horse
Grand dam: The grandmother of a horse
Colt: Young male horse, aged four and under
Gelding: Male horse that has been castrated
Stallion: Entire male horse that is mating mares
Filly: Female horse aged four and under
Mare: Female horse aged five and over
Juvenile: Youngest racehorse: on the flat a two-year-old, in jump racing a three/four-year-old
Maiden: A horse that has not yet won a race

THE FIRST LADY OF THE TURF

Queen Elizabeth, the Queen Mother, was affectionately known as "The First Lady of the Turf". Her passion for the sport began in 1949 when Lord Mildmay of Flete, the leading amateur jump jockey at the time, persuaded Queen Elizabeth to purchase a horse for her daughter, Princess Elizabeth (later Queen Elizabeth II), when he was staying with the Royal Family at Windsor Castle. In May 1994 she landed her 400th winner with Nearco Bay.

TREBLE OF WINS IN THE OAKS

Dermot Weld has trained the winner of the Oaks in three different countries:

- Oaks: Blue Wind – 1981
- Irish Oaks: Blue Wind – 1981, Dance Design – 1996
- American Oaks: Dimitrova – 2003

RACING SCANDALS (2)

On August Bank Holiday 1974 a horse named Gay Future was at the centre of an attempted coup by an Irish-based betting syndicate. The Irish horse was entered in a novice hurdle at Cartmel in what is now Cumbria. The trainer, Scottish-based Anthony Collins, had a poor-performing horse with that name at his yard. so bookmakers paid little attention to the Irish Gay Future and made him a 10-1 shot for the race. The "real" Gay Future was shipped over from Ireland and a lot of large bets involving doubles and trebles were placed on him, along with two guaranteed non-runners also trained by Collins – Opera Cloak and Ankerwyke – in an attempt to cover up the ruse. Opera Cloak and Ankerwyke had been entered in earlier races at different meetings that same day but were then withdrawn by Collins (in fact they never left their stables).

It must be remembered that in 1974 bookies didn't have modern technology, and coverage of race meetings, particularly those as remote as the Lake District, was almost non-existent. The last-minute withdrawals meant that all of the syndicate's bets, including the doubles and trebles, according to the rules of betting, rolled over onto Gay Future as a single bet. When Gay Future romped home by 15 lengths at 10-1, the bookmakers became suspicious of the unusual betting patterns.

A subsequent police investigation resulted in the trainer and the head of the Irish syndicate being convicted of conspiracy to defraud, but they escaped with small fines. The scam was dramatized in the 1979 made-for-TV movie *Murphy's Stoke*, starring Pierce Brosnan.

FIVEFORTHREE

Fiveforthree, ridden by Ruby Walsh, won the Ballymore Properties Novices' Hurdle at the 2008 Cheltenham Festival. "Fiveforthree" is a golfing term used in the Stableford points scoring format, meaning five shots on a hole that results in a net birdie.

FERDY MURPHY'S SCOTTISH HAT-TRICK

Ferdy Murphy has trained three winners of the Scottish Grand National: Paris Pike in 2000, Joes Edge in 2005 and Hot Weld in 2007. After landing the Scottish Grand National, Hot Weld went on to win the Ayr Gold Cup in the same year to become the only horse to do this unique double.

GUINEAS DOUBLE

Only four horses have ever achieved the 1000 and 2000 Guineas double, with Sceptre the last to achieve the feat in 1902. Amazingly, Sceptre is the only horse to win four of the five English Classics, adding the Oaks and the St Leger in 1902. She finished fourth in the 1902 Derby behind the winner Ard Patrick.

SCOTTISH NATIONAL SHOCK WIN

A major shock occurred at the 2008 Scottish Grand National when the 66-1 rank outsider, Iris de Balme, produced a superbly timed sprint finish to win the race, with Old Benny, the 4-1 favourite, fourth behind Halcon Genelardais and Flintoff. The Sean Curran-trained eight-year-old, 26 pounds out of the handicap, was ridden to victory by amateur rider Charlie Huxley, who sped past his opponents over the closing stages of the 4-mile race to win by a clear 14 lengths. Huxley is a former jockey who has ridden more than 100 winners and still holds a jockey's licence.

FINSCEAL BEO'S 1000 GUINEAS DOUBLE

In 2007 Finsceal Beo, ridden by Kevin Manning, trained by Jim Bolger and owned by Michael Ryan, won the 1000 Guineas to become only the second horse after Attraction in 2005 to complete the Double in the English and Irish Classics. She missed out on landing the Triple when she finished second to Darjina in the 2007 Poule d'Essai des Pouliches at Longchamp. Finsceal Beo is Irish for "Living Legend".

FOR THE GRANDCHILDREN

Aldaniti, winner of the 1981 Grand National, derived his name from the names of his breeder Tommy Barron's four grandchildren: Alastair, David, Nicola and Timothy.

ROCK OF GIBRALTAR

It should have been no surprise to anyone when Rock of Gibraltar, co-owned by Sir Alex Ferguson (the manager of Manchester United), won his first seven Group 1 races to set a new record. His sire was Danehill, Australian champion sire seven times, champion juvenile sire six times and champion European juvenile sire three times. Trainer Aidan O'Brien, in partnership with his wife, Anne-Marie, and father-in-law, John Crowley, covered his stable mare Offshore Boom with Danehill, and The Rock, as he became known, was foaled in 1999.

After winning five of his seven two-year-old outings, Rock of Gibraltar enjoyed an even better three-year-old campaign in Europe in 2002, finishing with the highest ever Timeform season rating of 133. Not surprisingly he was voted World Horse of the Year. His 13 career races produced ten wins and stakes prize-money of £1,164,804. In 2003 The Rock entered stud in Australia and Ireland, but not before the settlement of a long and drawn-out dispute of ownership of stud fees between Sir Alex Ferguson and the Coolmore Stud.

TAKING IT EASY

Throughout his riding career Lester Piggott battled to keep his weight down. Unusually tall for a jockey at 5ft 7½in, his diet in the lead-up to a race simply consisted of several small coffees, a few pieces of chocolate (Yorkie bars when they came out) and a few large cigars.

RACING AT CHELTENHAM ABANDONED

The second day of the 2008 Cheltenham Festival – Wednesday 12 March – had to be abandoned due to severe storms at the racecourse. Strong winds swirling around Prestbury Park had made the tented hospitality area unsafe and the course's Managing Director, Edward Gillespie, was forced to postpone racing. The races were all rescheduled for the Thursday and Friday, when the racecards comprised ten and nine races respectively.

YOUNGEST KENTUCKY DERBY WINNER

The 1892 Kentucky Derby was won by Azra, ridden by the African-American jockey Alonzo "Lonnie" Clayton. At just 15 years old, Clayton remains the youngest ever jockey to ride the winner of the Kentucky Derby.

HENRY CECIL

Henry Cecil's name is synonymous with the English Classics – it should be after landing 24 of them – and without question he is one of the greatest thoroughbred racehorse trainers of all time. Cecil was an out-and-out kingmaker, dominating the turf since acquiring his licence in 1969. His CV is the envy of the horse-racing world. He has won every English Classic and more than once: 1000 Guineas – six times, 2000 Guineas – twice, St Leger – four times, Oaks – eight times and the Derby – four times. His impressive tally of 34 Classics at home and abroad (up to the end of June 2008) also saw him saddle some of the greatest jockeys the sport has ever seen including Joe Mercer, Pat Eddery, Steve Cauthen, Kieren Fallon, Frankie Dettori and perhaps the best of them all, Lester Piggott.

He claimed the title of Champion Trainer 10 times – 1976, 1978, 1979, 1982, 1984, 1985, 1987, 1988, 1990 and 1993. He is an icon of the sport and is one of the few trainers who can claim legendary status over any of the horses that he has trained at his Warren Place Stables.

SANTA CLAUS WINS THE DERBY

Santa Claus won the Derby in 1964 ridden by Scobie Breasley and trained by Mick Rogers. He also won the National Stakes (1963), the Irish Derby Stakes (1964), the Irish 2000 Guineas (1964) and finished runner-up in the King George VI and Queen Elizabeth Diamond Stakes (1964) and the Prix de l'Arc de Triomphe (1964).

CARL'S DOUBLE

Run For Paddy won the 2006 Scottish Grand National and was both trained and ridden by Carl Llewellyn.

THE HORSE WITH NO EQUAL

In 29 successive races between October 1962 and December 1966 the legendary steeplechaser Arkle was defeated only four times: after slipping on landing over the third last fence in the 1963 Hennessy Gold Cup; in the 1964 Massey-Ferguson and 1966 Hennessy Gold Cup when the weight he was asked to carry was simply too much for him; and finally in the 1966 King George VI Chase after galloping around Kempton Park for 2 miles with a broken pedal bone.

O'BRIEN ON HIS WAY

In 1958 Ballymoss, trained by Vincent O'Brien, owned by John McShain and ridden by Scobie Breasley, became the first English Classic winner to win the Prix de l'Arc de Triomphe. He won the 1957 St Leger ridden by Tommy Burns, O'Brien's first Classic success. In his career Ballymoss set a new UK prize money record.

RACING JARGON (4)

Plate – racehorses wear special shoes for racing named "racing plates". A horse that loses a shoe is said to have spread a plate.

BRITISH RACECOURSES

In April 2008 Great Leighs became the 60th racecourse in Britain:

Aintree	*Ascot*	*Ayr*	**Bangor on Dee**
Bath	Beverley	Brighton	*Carlisle*
Cartmel	*Catterick*	**Cheltenham**	*Chepstow*
Chester	*Doncaster*	Epsom	**Exeter**
Fakenham	*Folkestone*	**Fontwell Park**	Goodwood
Great Leighs*	Hamilton	*Haydock Park*	**Hereford**
Hexham	**Huntingdon**	**Kelso**	*Kempton Park**
Leicester	*Lingfield Park**	**Ludlow**	**Market Rasen**
Newbury	*Newcastle*	Newmarket	**Newton Abbot**
Musselburgh	Nottingham	**Perth**	**Plumpton**
Pontefract	Redcar	Ripon	Salisbury
Sandown Park	**Sedgfield**	*Southwell**	**Stratford upon Avon**
Taunton	Thirsk	**Towcester**	**Uttoxeter**
Warwick	**Wetherby**	**Wincanton**	Windsor
Wolverhampton*	**Worcester**	Yarmouth	York

Flat only, unless **Bold = NH only**; *Italic = dual purpose*; * = all-weather

FAN MAIL

Arkle used to receive letters from adoring fans around the world simply addressed to "Arkle, Ireland". The story goes that one little boy wrote a letter to Arkle's owner, Anne, Duchess of Westminster, in which he wrote, "Dear Duchess, I would like to buy Arkle because my dog has just died. I have 7s 6d and some Superman comics." Hundreds of other letters asked for the horse's autograph and he was sent presents on a daily basis, including carrots, sugar lumps and his favourite tipple, Guinness.

CHAMPION FLAT TRAINERS 1945–2008

In both flat and National Hunt racing, the trainers' championship is not decided on the number of race wins, but on the amount of prize money earned by the horses trained at the stable:

2008	A.P. O'Brien	1976	H. Cecil
2007	A.P. O'Brien	1975	P. Walwyn
2006	Sir M. Stoute	1974	P. Walwyn
2005	Sir M. Stoute	1973	C.F.N. Murless
2004	Saeed Bin Suroor	1972	W. Hern
2003	Sir M. Stoute	1971	I. Balding
2002	A.P. O'Brien	1970	C.F.N. Murless
2001	A.P. O'Brien	1969	A.M. Budgett
2000	Sir M. Stoute	1968	C.F.N. Murless
1999	Saeed Bin Suroor	1967	C.F.N. Murless
1998	Saeed Bin Suroor	1966	M.V. O'Brien
1997	M. Stoute	1965	P.J. Prendergast
1996	Saeed Bin Suroor	1964	P.J. Prendergast
1995	J. Dunlop	1963	P.J. Prendergast
1994	M. Stoute	1962	W. Hern
1993	H. Cecil	1961	C.F.N. Murless
1992	R. Hannon	1960	C.F.N. Murless
1991	P. Cole	1959	C.F.N. Murless
1990	H. Cecil	1958	C. Boyd-Rochfort
1989	M. Stoute	1957	C.F.N. Murless
1988	H. Cecil	1956	C.F. Elsey
1987	H Cecil	1955	C. Boyd-Rochfort
1986	M. Stoute	1954	C. Boyd-Rochfort
1985	H. Cecil	1953	J.L. Jarvis
1984	H. Cecil	1952	M. Marsh
1983	W. Hern	1951	J.L. Jarvis
1982	H. Cecil	1950	C.H. Semblat
1981	M. Stoute	1949	F. Butters
1980	W. Hern	1948	C.F.N. Murless
1979	H. Cecil	1947	F. Darling
1978	H. Cecil	1946	F. Butters
1977	M.V. O'Brien	1945	W. Earl

Did You Know That?
France's Charles Semblat trained the winner of the Oaks, Derby and St Leger in 1950, making him Britain's leading trainer although he never set foot on British soil.

CHAMPION JUMP TRAINERS 1945–2008

2007–08 P. Nicholls
2006–07 P. Nicholls
2005–06 P. Nicholls
2004–05 M. Pipe
2003–04 M. Pipe
2002–03 M. Pipe
2001–02 M. Pipe
2000–01 M. Pipe
1999–00 M. Pipe
1998–99 M. Pipe
1997–98 M. Pipe
1996–97 M. Pipe
1995–96 M. Pipe
1994–95 D. Nicholson
1993–94 D. Nicholson
1992–93 M. Pipe
1991–92 M. Pipe
1990–91 M. Pipe
1989–90 M. Pipe
1988–89 M. Pipe
1987–88 D.R.C. Elsworth
1986–87 N.J. Henderson
1985–86 N.J. Henderson
1984–85 F.T. Winter
1983–84 M.W. Dickinson
1982–83 M.W. Dickinson
1981–82 M.W. Dickinson
1980–81 M.H. Easterby
1979–80 M.H. Easterby
1978–79 M.H. Easterby
1977–78 F.T. Winter
1976–77 F.T. Winter
1975–76 T.F. Rimell
1974–75 F.T. Winter
1973–74 F.T. Winter
1972–73 F.T. Winter
1971–72 F.T. Winter
1970–71 F.T. Winter
1969–70 TF. Rimell
1968–69 T.F. Rimell
1967–68 D. Smith
1966–67 R. Price
1965–66 R. Price
1964–65 P.V.F. Cazalet
1963–64 F. Walwyn
1962–63 K. Piggott
1961–62 R. Price
1960–61 T.F. Rimell
1959–60 P.V.F. Cazalet
1958–59 R. Price
1957–58 F. Walwyn
1956–57 N. Crump
1955–56 W Hall
1954–55 R. Price
1953–54 M.V. O'Brien
1952–53 M.V. O'Brien
1951–52 N. Crump
1950–51 T.F. Rimell
1949–50 P.V.F. Cazalet
1948–49 F. Walwyn
1947–48 F. Walwyn
1946–47 F. Walwyn
1945–46 T. Rayson

THE CHAIR

The Chair, the famous fence jumped in the Grand National at Aintree, got its name from the fact that the fence was situated alongside the seat occupied by the distance judge. It is the biggest fence in the National, standing an awesome 1.55 metres (5 feet 2 inches) tall and 1.8 metres (6 feet) wide. The landing side is higher than the take-off.

ADRIAN'S SCOTTISH DOUBLE

Adrian Maguire is the only jockey to win two Scottish Grand Nationals. He won in 1998 on the David Nicholson-trained Baronet and again in 2000 on the Ferdy Murphy-trained Paris Pike.

DERBY USES FIRST STARTING GATE

A mechanical starting gate was introduced for the first time in 1901 and it was first operated for the Derby at Epsom.

RACING JARGON (5)

Furlong – the unit of distance used in British horse racing. A furlong measures 1/8 of a mile, which is 220 yards or approximately 200m.

THE WIZARD FROM OZ

The Australian jockey, Edgar Britt, won back-to-back St Legers in 1947 (Sayajirao) and 1948 (Black Tarquin). He won his first Classic, the Irish Derby in 1947, on Sayajirao which was owned by the Maharajah of Baroda. In 1949 he won the 1000 Guineas and Oaks with Musidora, the 1952 Oaks with Frieze, the 2000 Guineas in 1953 with Nearula and the 1000 Guineas in 1956 with Honeylight, all for Charles Elsey's stable. In 2004, aged 90, Britt was inducted into the Australian Racing Hall of Fame.

FROM THE HORSE'S MOUTH (3)

"One of the grandest sights in racing has always been to see Lester [Piggott] hauled before the stewards. He goes in there like Clint Eastwood, and he comes out like Clint Eastwood. Lester doesn't give a monkey's."
***Bryn Crossley**, jockey*

GOLD CUP BONANZA

Bookmakers announced record takings for Gold Cup day at the 2008 Cheltenham Festival after some £300 million was staked on the racing with a staggering £3.87 million bet on the course alone. David Williams from Ladbrokes said, "Today's takings have dwarfed the Grand National and the FA Cup final. It's been an incredible day for the industry."

SCOBIE BREASLEY

Australia's Arthur Edward "Scobie" Breasley was one of the leading jockeys of the post-war era. He was born on 14 May 1914 in Wagga Wagga, New South Wales. Scobie left school aged 12 and worked in local stables near his home before being appointed an apprentice to the Melbourne trainer Pat Quinlan. In 1926, aged just 14, he rode his first winner, Noogee, at Weribee, Victoria.

After winning all there was to win in Australia (he was Champion Jockey of Victoria four times and won four consecutive Caulfield Cups – 1942–45), with the notable exception of the Melbourne Cup (despite 16 attempts), he packed his bags and headed for England in 1950. He was invited to England by J.V. Rank, a flour millionaire and racehorse owner, to ride as his Druids Lodge Stables' (on Salisbury Plain) jockey to his trainer Noel Cannon. After two unsuccessful years in Wiltshire, Breasley and his homesick wife returned to Australia where he won a fifth Caulfield Cup in 1952. He returned to England in 1953 at the invitation of "Lucky" Jack Dewar, a millionaire whisky distiller. Dewar bought the Breasleys a house in Putney, London, which remained their home for more than 30 years.

In 1954 he landed his first English Classic, winning the 1000 Guineas on Dewar's filly, Festoon, but shortly after his Newmarket glory Breasley fell at the now closed Alexandra Park. He fractured his skull and both of his eyes were paralyzed, causing him to lose his sense of balance. Doctors told him that he was lucky to still be alive and advised him not to ride again, but the tough Aussie was having none of it. Breasley played a round of golf every day with his fellow countryman, professional golfer Norman van Nida, and regained his balance. Amazingly he was back in the saddle after just 12 weeks.

Breasley won the Jockeys' Championship on four occasions (1957 and 1961–63 inclusive), the last of them at the age of 49. He landed four Classics and also won numerous other Group 1 races, including the Prix de l'Arc de Triomphe, on Ballymoss for Irish trainer Vincent O'Brien, in 1958.

Scobie retired in 1968 after having ridden a total of 3,251 winners worldwide (2,161 in Britain) to take up training. He was the first inductee into the Australian Racing Hall of Fame in 2001. Breasley died, aged 92, on 21 December 2006 after suffering a stroke.

Did You Know That?

He got his nickname, "Scobie", from his adulation of the top Australian trainer Jim Scobie.

OAKS WINNERS 1946–2008

Year	*Winner*	*Jockey*	*Trainer*
2008	Look Here	Seb Sanders	Ralph Beckett
2007	Light Shift	Ted Durcan	Henry Cecil
2006	Alexandrova	Kieren Fallon	Aidan O'Brien
2005	Eswarah	Richard Hills	Michael Jarvis
2004	Ouija Board	Kieren Fallon	Ed Dunlop
2003	Casual Look	Martin Dwyer	Andrew Balding
2002	Kazzia	Frankie Dettori	Saeed bin Suroor
2001	Imagine	Michael Kinane	Aidan O'Brien
2000	Love Divine	Richard Quinn	Henry Cecil
1999	Ramruma	Kieren Fallon	Henry Cecil
1998	Shahtoush	Michael Kinane	Aidan O'Brien
1997	Reams of Verse	Kieren Fallon	Henry Cecil
1996	Lady Carla	Pat Eddery	Henry Cecil
1995	Moonshell	Frankie Dettori	Saeed bin Suroor
1994	Balanchinev	Frankie Dettori	Hilal Ibrahim
1993	Intrepidity	Michael Roberts	André Fabre
1992	User Friendly	George Duffield	Clive Brittain
1991	Jet Ski Lady	Christy Roche	Jim Bolger
1990	Salsabil	Willie Carson	John Dunlop
1989	Snow Bride *	Steve Cauthen	Henry Cecil
1988	Diminuendo	Steve Cauthen	Henry Cecil
1987	Unitev	Walter Swinburn	Michael Stoute
1986	Midway Lady	Ray Cochrane	Ben Hanbury
1985	Oh So Sharp	Steve Cauthen	Henry Cecil
1984	Circus Plume	Lester Piggott	John Dunlop
1983	Sun Princess	Willie Carson	Dick Hern
1982	Time Charter	Billy Newnes	Henry Candy
1981	Blue Wind	Lester Piggott	Dermot Weld
1980	Bireme	Willie Carson	Dick Hern
1979	Scintillate	Pat Eddery	Jeremy Tree
1978	Fair Salinia	Greville Starkey	Michael Stoute
1977	Dunfermline	Willie Carson	Dick Hern
1976	Pawneese	Yves Saint-Martin	Angel Penna Sr
1975	Juliette Marny	Lester Piggott	Jeremy Tree
1974	Polygamy	Pat Eddery	Peter Walwyn
1973	Mysterious	Geoff Lewis	Noel Murless
1972	Ginerva	Tony Murray	Ryan Price
1971	Altesse Royale	Geoff Lewis	Noel Murless
1970	Lupe	Sandy Barclay	Noel Murless
1969	Sleeping Partner	John Gorton	Doug Smith

1968	La Lagune	Gerard Thiboeuf	François Boutin
1967	Pia	Eddie Hide	Bill Elsey
1966	Valoris	Lester Piggott	Vincent O'Brien
1965	Long Look	Jack Purtell	Vincent O'Brien
1964	Homeward Bound	Greville Starkey	John Oxley
1963	Noblesse	Garnie Bougoure	Paddy Prendergast
1962	Monade	Yves Saint-Martin	Joseph Lieux
1961	Sweet Solera	Bill Rickaby	Reginald Day
1960	Never Too Late II	Roger Poincelet	Etienne Pollet
1959	Petite Etoile	Lester Piggott	Noel Murless
1958	Bella Paola	Max Garcia	François Mathet
1957	Carrozza	Lester Piggott	Noel Murless
1956	Sicarelle	Freddie Palmer	François Mathet
1955	Meld	Harry Carr	Cecil Boyd-Rochfort
1954	Sun Cap	Rae Johnstone	Dick Carver
1953	Ambiguity	Joe Mercer	Jack Colling
1952	Frieze	Edgar Britt	Charles Elsey
1951	Neasham Belle	Stan Clayton	Geoffrey Brooke
1950	Asmena	Rae Johnstone	Charles Semblat
1949	Musidora	Edgar Britt	Charles Elsey
1948	Masaka	Billy Nevett	Frank Butters
1947	Imprudence	Rae Johnstone	Joseph Lieux
1946	Steady Aim	Harry Wragg	Frank Butters

* *Aliysa finished first in 1989 but was subsequently disqualified after testing positive for a banned substance.*

THE HEAVYWEIGHTS

Since the end of the Second World War only five Grand Nationals have been won by horses carrying more than 11 stone 5 pounds, with Red Rum doing it twice.

VICTORIOUS KING

King George VI's Big Game won the 2000 Guineas in 1942, ridden by Gordon Richards and trained by Fred Darling.

BRITAIN 18 IRELAND 7

Over the three days of racing at the 2008 Cheltenham Festival, British horses won 18 of the 25 races at the festival, with Ireland claiming the remaining 7.

CITATION

Citation was foaled on 11 April 1945, sired by Bull Lea (one of the greatest sires in thoroughbred breeding history) out of Hydroplane. His paternal grandsire was Bull Dog, the leading sire in North America in 1953, 1954 and 1956. Bull Dog's progeny included horses that won 52 stakes races. His paternal damsire was the legendary Hyperion, winner of the Derby and St Leger in 1933.

The horse, a bay colt, was owned and bred by Calumet Farm in Lexington, Kentucky, and trained by the Hall of Fame father and son trainers Ben and Horace "Jimmy" Jones. On 22 April 1947, the two-year-old won at the first time of asking at the Havre de Grace track in Maryland. In his second outing Citation broke the Arlington Park track record over 5 furlongs. He raced nine times as a two-year-old and only lost once, to stablemate Bewitch. With earnings of $155,680, Citation was named champion two-year-old.

Citation was even more impressive as a three-year-old, beginning 1948 with a win over the 1947 Horse of the Year, Armed. As a two-year-old Citation had been ridden by Al Snider or Steve Brooks but in 1948 Eddie Arcaro took over. They lost to Saggy in the Chesapeake Trial Stakes in Arcaro's first race aboard, but it would be his last for nearly two years. The pair eased to victory in the 1948 Kentucky Derby, 3½ lengths clear of the field. Next up for Citation was the Preakness Stakes at Baltimore where he won by 5½ lengths. At Elmont Park, New York, Citation became only the eighth US Triple Crown winner in history, winning the race by 8 lengths and equalling the Belmont Stakes record time of 2:28.20.

From mid-April 1948 to mid-January 1950, Citation won a record 16 consecutive major races (including 13 Stakes). Amazingly, such was his superiority that no other horse was prepared to race Citation in the 1948 Pimlico Special, so he was forced to race alone. By the end of his three-year-old season, Citation had a career record of 27 victories and two seconds in 29 starts, with prize money of $865,150. He was named Horse of the Year for 1948.

Citation missed the 1949 season with an ankle injury but as a five-year-old he set a new world record time for the mile. After winning the 1951 Hollywood Gold Cup as a six-year-old, bringing his career earnings over the $1 million mark, he was sent to stud. In total he had 32 wins, ten second places and two thirds in his 45 starts.

Did You Know That?

Citation went off as the favourite in 43 of his 44 races where betting took place.

NEW DERBY STAKES

The Derby's popularity was such that it ran uninterrupted during both world wars. However, from 1915 to 1918 the race took place at Newmarket and was called the New Derby Stakes.

THE DEVON LOCH MYSTERY

In the 1956 Grand National Devon Loch, ridden by Dick Francis and owned by the Queen Mother, was well clear of the field after jumping the last hurdle and then inexplicably the horse tried to jump a non-existent fence and flopped on to his belly. Apparently Devon Loch thought a shadow on the course cast by the grandstand was a fence and as he lay on the turf ESB ran past him to win.

RACING SCANDALS (3)

In August 1978, In The Money won the Hatherleigh Selling Handicap Hurdle at Newton Abbot by 20 lengths priced at 8-1. He had been well backed but it was soon discovered that he was actually the five-times winner Cobbler's March. When the police visited trainer John Bowles' yard, In The Money had been destroyed owing to "lameness". Bowles was jailed for 18 months.

RACING JARGON (6)

Place bet – a punter who is not certain his selection will win the race can bet on the horse being placed. Depending on the number of runners, bets will be paid out on horses finishing first or second where there are 5–7 runners, first, second or third if eight or more run, and – in handicaps – first, second, third or fourth, if there are a minimum of 16 at the off. If there are four runners or fewer, then only win bets can be made. As there is a much better chance of a place bet winning, they are settled at a fifth or a quarter of the advertised price. A winning 5-1 place bet at a quarter of the odds will pay at 1.25-1.

BARBARO BREAKS DOWN

On 20 May 2006, Barbaro, winner of the 2006 Kentucky Derby, and 1-2 favourite for the Preakness Stakes at Pimlico, broke down with a fractured leg early in the race. Although the horse underwent numerous surgeries, he developed laminitis and eventually was put down on 29 January 2007.

A KING'S RANSOM

When Priam, ridden by Sam Day and trained by William Chifney, won the 1830 Derby it was worth £2,800 to his connections, which at the time was a king's ransom. To compare, New Approach, trained by Jim Bolger and ridden by Kevin Manning, netted a cool £802,453 for his connections upon winning the 2008 race.

THE CAPTAIN

Tim Forster, OBE (affectionately known as "The Captain" after serving with the 11th Hussars), saddled three Aintree Grand National winners. His first victory in the race came in 1972 with Well To Do, ridden by Graham Thorner. Forster was a renowned pessimist and only made the decision to allow Well To Do to run 15 minutes before the race. In 1980 he landed his second National with Ben Nevis, partnered by the amateur jockey Charlie Fenwick who he told before the race to "just keep remounting". His final win came in 1985 with Last Suspect, ridden by Hywel Davies. Forster hated hurdles and flat racing so much he often said that if he ever became an MP one of the first things he would do would be to outlaw both of them. Forster trained 1,346 winners during his 36-year training career, retiring in June 1998. He died on 21 April 1999.

FROM THE HORSE'S MOUTH (4)

"Certain races come in and out of fashion. But the Derby is quite unique. I don't think it will ever go out of fashion. It is the race I always wanted to win the most and I think most trainers would agree. There is so much prestige attached to it."
Vincent O'Brien*, trainer of six Derby winners*

LITERARY SUCCESS

When the racing career of 1953–54 champion jump jockey Dick Francis came to an end he became a successful author. He famously led in the 1956 Grand National, aboard the Queen Mother's Devon Loch, but the horse stumbled on the run-in.

ON AN EQUAL FOOTING

Since 2001, the winning prize money for the 2000 Guineas and the 1000 Guineas has been the same. In 2008, it was £375,000.

200TH 2000 GUINEAS

In 2008 Henrythenavigator, ridden by Johnny Murtagh and trained by Aidan O'Brien, won the 2000 Guineas. O'Brien's success was the Irish trainer's third victory in the race in the last four years, and the fourth of his career to draw level with his namesake and the man he succeeded at Ballydoyle Stables, the legendary Vincent O'Brien. The trainer said of Henrythenavigator, "He's a proper high-class, fast-ground miler. He's always shown us that at home, but when he got beaten last year it was on National Hunt ground. And after that we went easy on him, didn't push him, so we'd have him for this year. And Johnny [Murtagh] played the horse to all his strengths." Aidan O'Brien's other winners were Rock of Gibraltar (2002), Footstepsinthesand (2005) and George Washington (2006). The inaugural race was won in 1809 by Wizard, ridden by Bill Clift and trained by Tom Perren.

THE VOICE OF RACING

Sir Peter O'Sullevan, KBE, was born on 3 March 1918 in Kenmare, County Kerry, Ireland. During the late 1940s he gave some of the earliest television commentaries on various sports and also commentated on the Grand National for radio before the famous Aintree steeplechase was televised live for the first time in 1960. Universally recognized as "the voice of racing", commentating on all of the big races including the Cheltenham Festival, the Grand National, the Prix de l'Arc de Triomphe, the Derby, Glorious Goodwood and Royal Ascot, O'Sullevan commentated on his 50th and final Grand National in 1997. In an interview before to the race he revealed that his commentary binoculars came from a German submarine. He was knighted the same year, the only sports broadcaster at the time to receive the prestigious award.

He was also a successful racehorse owner, including Be Friendly who won the King's Stand Stakes at Ascot and the Prix de l'Abbaye at Longchamps. In 1974 he commentated on the Triumph Hurdle at the Cheltenham Festival with his own horse, Attivo, running in it. Just as Attivo crossed the line to win O'Sullevan quite casually said, "And it's first Attivo, trained by Cyril Mitchel, ridden by Robert Hughes and owned by Peter O'Sullevan." Since his retirement, O'Sullevan has been actively involved in charity work, fund-raising for causes including the International League for the Protection of Horses. At the 2008 Cheltenham Festival, the National Hunt Challenge Chase Cup was named after him to celebrate his 90th birthday.

RIMELL'S NATIONAL

The name "Rimell" has appeared on the Grand National Roll of Honour five times. Trainer Tom Rimell won with Forbra in 1932, while his son Fred is the only trainer in the race's history to train four different winners: ESB (1956), Nicolaus Silver (1961), Gay Trip (1970) and Rag Trade (1976).

KEEP YOUR TROUSERS ON

Just as Nijinsky romped home to victory in the 1970 Derby his owner, Charles Engelhard Jr, celebrated so enthusiastically that his braces snapped. In an interview with the *Times Online*, Nijinksy's trainer Vincent O'Brien recalled the moment it happened: "When Charles went up to the Royal Box to meet the Queen Mother, he held his pants up with his elbows. He had his walking stick in one hand and his top hat in the other, prompting the Queen Mother to ask if she could hold anything for him. Charles said afterwards that if he'd moved his arms his trousers would have fallen down by his ankles."

STEP BY STEP

One month before the running of the Grand National the race organizers begin building the fences. The spruce for the fences is sourced and transported from the Lake District and costs approximately £20,000.

RACING JARGON (7)

Novice – a term used in jump racing. A novice hurdler is a horse that has not won a hurdle race before the current jump season begins, whereas a novice chaser is a horse that has not won a steeplechase before the current jump season begins.

KING GEORGE VI CHASE

The King George VI Chase is a Grade 1 race, open to horses aged four years and above, run over a distance of 3 miles at Kempton Park, usually on Boxing Day. There are 18 fences to negotiate (it was 19 until 2005, when the water jump was removed during racecourse redevelopment). The inaugural King George was run in February 1937 in honour of Britain's new monarch, King George VI, and was won by Southern Hero, who, aged 12, remains the race's oldest ever winner.

2008 CARTIER AWARDS

The Cartier Awards are British horse racing's top prize-giving ceremony for the horses. Started in 1991, they recognize the leading performers in flat racing and are voted upon by journalists and readers of the *Racing Post* and the *Daily Telegraph*. The 2008 Prix de l'Arc de Triomphe winner Zarkava won the prestigious Horse of the Year award at the 2008 Cartier Racing Awards, held in London on 17 November 2007. The three-year-old Irish bred filly, trained in France by Alain de Royer-Dupre and owned and bred by HH The Aga Khan, won the Arc, having already claimed the French 1000 Guineas and Oaks (Poule d'Essai des Pouliches and Prix du Diane, respectively).

The Ballydoyle stables of Aidan O'Brien claimed three of the awards, Top Older Horse, Top Stayer and Two-year-old Colt. The only human award is the special Cartier/Daily Telegraph Award of Merit, selected by a jury of 20 judges, and the 2008 recipient was Sheikh Mohammed bin Rashid Al Maktoum, the founder of the Godolphin training operation.

2008 WINNERS

Horse of the Year	Zarkava
Top Older Horse	Duke of Marmalade
Top Stayer	Yeats
Top Sprinter	Marchand d'Or
Three-year-old Colt	New Approach
Three-year-old Filly	Zarkava
Two-year-old Colt	Mastercraftsman
Two-year-old Filly	Rainbow View
Award of Merit	Sheikh Mohammed

QUICKEST EVER OAKS

In 1993 Intrepidity, ridden by Michael Roberts, trained by André Fabre and owned by Sheikh Mohammed, won the Oaks in the fastest ever time – 2 minutes, 34.19 seconds.

JIMMY'S FIRST

In 2007 jockey Jimmy Fortune claimed his first Classic success when he rode Lucarno to victory in the St Leger. The John Gosden-trained colt was fourth in the 2007 Derby before winning York's Great Voltigeur a few weeks before his Doncaster glory.

100-1 DERBY WINNERS

The three longest-priced Derby winners all started the Classic at 100-1: Jeddah in 1898, Signorinetta in 1908 and Aboyeur in 1913.

EARTH SUMMIT'S UNIQUE TREBLE

On 4 April 1998, Earth Summit, ridden by Carl Llwellyn and trained by Nigel Twiston-Davies, jumped his way into racing's history books when he won the Grand National at Aintree. His win meant that he became the first horse ever to land the Scottish (1994), Welsh (1997) and English Grand Nationals, a feat even the legendary Red Rum could not achieve. In total he won 10 races earning £420,000 in prize money.

BACK-TO-BACK 2000 GUINEAS TREBLES

The last time the 2000 Guineas trio of owner, trainer and jockey claimed back-to-back wins in the Classic was when Footstepsinthesand won in 2005 followed by George Washington in 2006. Kieren Fallon rode both winners, saddled by Aidan O'Brien, while Sue Magnier and Michael Tabor owned both horses (Footstepsinthesand together and George Washington in partnership Derrick Smith).

LUCKY NINES

Nine-year-olds have proved the most successful age group in recent years in the Grand National, with nine of the last 30 winners being that age: Lucius (1978), Grittar (1982), West Tip (1986), Rhyme 'N' Reason (1988), Lord Gyllene (1997), Bobbyjo (1999), Papillon (2000), Hedgehunter (2005) and the 2008 winner, Comply Or Die.

500-1 SHOT SECOND IN THE DERBY

In 1989 the Clive Brittain-trained Terimon came second to the 5-4 favourite Nashwan in the Derby. Terimon ws priced at 500-1 and remains the longest-priced placed horse in the race's history.

BREED REGISTRY

Since 1793, members of the Weatherby family have been responsible for every subsequent volume of the *General Stud Book*.

♀

1000 GUINEAS STATISTICS

Leading jockey – seven wins
George Fordham – Mayonaise (1859), Nemesis (1861), Siberia (1865), Formosa (1868), Scottish Queen (1869), Thebais (1881), Hauteur (1883)
Leading trainer – nine wins
Robert Robson – Corinne (1818), Catgut (1819), Rowena (1820), Zeal (1821), Whizgig (1822), Zinc (1823), Tontine (1825), Problem (1826), Arab (1827)
Leading owner – eight wins
4th Duke of Grafton – Catgut (1819), Rowena (1820), Zeal (1821), Whizgig (1822), Zinc (1823), Tontine (1825), Problem (1826), Arab (1827)
Fastest winning time – Finsceal Beo (2007), 1 minute 34.94 seconds
Widest winning margin (since 1900) – Humble Duty (1970) 7 lengths
Longest-odds winner – Ferry 50-1 (1918)
Shortest-odds winner – Crucifix 1-10 (1840)
Most runners – 29 in 1926
Fewest runners – 1 (a walkover) in 1825

RACING JARGON (8)

Jackpot – a Tote bet, where the punter has to select the winner of each of six preselected races. The Scoop6 is the biggest jackpot pool and takes place every Saturday.

FROM THE HORSE'S MOUTH (5)

"I've got a nasty bang at the top of my mouth and they think I might have a small fracture of the gum, but you forget pain when you ride winners. My face could have been broken to bits and I would have come out to ride this lad. I love the horse."
***Tony McCoy**, after riding Black Jack Ketchum to victory at Cheltenham in December 2005*

OAKS BY A DISTANCE

In 1983 Sun Princess, ridden by Willie Carson, trained by Major Dick Hern and owned by Sir Michael Sobell, won the Oaks by the biggest ever margin – 10 lengths

PHOTO-FINISH DERBY

In 1949 the Derby was decided by a photo-finish camera for the first time, with Nimbus ridden by Charlie Elliott declared the winner.

OLD BOY LANDS THE NATIONAL

In 1982 48-year-old Dick Saunders became the oldest jockey to win the Grand National after steering Grittar to victory at Aintree. Amazingly it was his first and only ever ride in the race. The late Frank Gilman, Grittar's trainer, remains the last permit-holder to train the winner of the Grand National and Saunders became the only member of the Jockey Club to ride a National winner.

MOVIE POPCORN

Popcorn Deelites, a horse in Northern Dancer's bloodline, has a claim to fame: he played Seabiscuit in most of the scenes in the 2003 movie of the same name. In his racing career, Popcorn Deelites won 11 times in 58 mainly small races earning almost $60,000 in prize money.

DANCING BRAVE

In 1986 Dancing Brave, ridden by Greville Starkey and trained by Guy Harwood, won the 2000 Guineas and that same year the horse also won the Craven Stakes (Greville Starkey), Eclipse Stakes (Greville Starkey), King George VI and Queen Elizabeth Diamond Stakes (Pat Eddery), Select Stakes (Greville Starkey) and the Prix de l'Arc de Triomphe (Pat Eddery).

COCKNEY REBEL'S 2000 GUINEAS DOUBLE

In 2007 Cockney Rebel, ridden by Olivier Peslier, trained by Geoff Huffer and owned by Phil Cunningham, became the first horse since Rock of Gibraltar in 2002 to complete the double in the English and Irish 2000 Guineas. The horse was a 25-1 outsider to win the race at Newmarket.

ENGLAND'S KENTUCKY DERBY RAIDERS

Only two English-bred horses have won the Kentucky Derby – Omar Khayyam in 1917 (the first foreign-bred horse to win the race) and Tomy Lee in 1959.

CARRIED AWAY

Only three horses have carried 12 stone or more to victory in the Hennessy Cognac Gold Cup: Arkle (1964 and 1965 carrying 12 stone 7 pounds), Mill House (1963 carrying 12 stone) and Burrough Hill Lad (1984 carrying 12 stone).

THE MARYLAND HUNT CUP

The Maryland Hunt Cup is the most prestigious steeplechase in the USA. However, unlike the hedge fences in the Aintree Grand National the fences in the Maryland Hunt Cup are solid wooden fences with the top rail firmly nailed down. The race is run at Worthington Valley racecourse situated on the outskirts of Baltimore, Maryland. The inaugural Maryland Hunt Cup was held in 1894 when two rival fox hunt clubs (The Elkridge Fox Hunting Club and the Green Spring Valley Hounds) challenged one another to see which had the best horses. The inaugural race was limited to members of the two clubs but in 1895 the race was opened to all fox hunting clubs in Maryland. Then in 1903, members from recognized clubs across the USA and Canada were invited to participate. The Maryland Hunt Cup is open to amateur riders only.

WHERE DID YOU GET THAT HAT?

Ladies' Day at Royal Ascot is one of the most colourful spectacles in the world of thoroughbred horse racing. Ladies' Day is traditionally Gold Cup day, where many spectators turn their attention from the racing to fashion and in particular the array of weird and wonderful hats that adorn the heads of the ladies in the various enclosures and boxes around the course. Indeed, many of the ladies' modern millinery manages to outshine the rich and colourful silks worn by the jockeys.

FIRST LADY OF ROYAL ASCOT

In 1970 Rosemary Lomax became the first woman trainer to win the Ascot Gold Cup when Precipice Wood ridden by Jimmy Lindley landed her the victory.

WELLES MOVIE

In 1970, a movie entitled *A Horse Called Nijinsky* was made and narrated by Orson Welles.

DERBY WINNERS 1946–2008

Year	*Winner*	*Jockey*	*Trainer*
2008	New Approach	Kevin Manning	Jim Bolger
2007	Authorized	Frankie Dettori	Peter Chapple-Hyam
2006	Sir Percy	Martin Dwyer	Marcus Tregoning
2005	Motivator	Johnny Murtagh	Michael Bell
2004	North Light	Kieren Fallon	Sir Michael Stoute
2003	Kris Kin	Kieren Fallon	Sir Michael Stoute
2002	High Chaparral	Johnny Murtagh	Aidan O'Brien
2001	Galileo	Michael Kinane	Aidan O'Brien
2000	Sinndar	Johnny Murtagh	John Oxx
1999	Oath	Kieren Fallon	Henry Cecil
1998	High-Rise	Olivier Peslier	Luca Cumani
1997	Benny the Dip	Willie Ryan	John Gosden
1996	Shaamit	Michael Hills	William Haggas
1995	Lammtarra	Walter Swinburn	Saeed bin Suroor
1994	Erhaab	Willie Carson	John Dunlop
1993	Commander in Chief	Michael Kinane	Henry Cecil
1992	Dr Devious	John Reid	Peter Chapple-Hyam
1991	Generous	Alan Munro	Paul Cole
1990	Quest For Fame	Pat Eddery	Roger Charlton
1989	Nashwan	Willie Carson	Dick Hern
1988	Kahyasi	Ray Cochrane	Luca Cumani
1987	Reference Point	Steve Cauthen	Henry Cecil
1986	Shahrastani	Walter Swinburn	Michael Stoute
1985	Slip Anchor	Steve Cauthen	Henry Cecil
1984	Secreto	Christy Roche	David O'Brien
1983	Teenoso	Lester Piggott	Geoff Wragg
1982	Golden Fleece	Pat Eddery	Vincent O'Brien
1981	Shergar	Walter Swinburn	Michael Stoute
1980	Henbit	Willie Carson	Dick Hern
1979	Troy	Willie Carson	Dick Hern
1978	Shirley Heights	Greville Starkey	John Dunlop
1977	The Minstrel	Lester Piggott	Vincent O'Brien
1976	Empery	Lester Piggott	Maurice Zilber
1975	Grundy	Pat Eddery	Peter Walwyn
1974	Snow Knight	Brian Taylor	Peter Nelson
1973	Morston	Eddie Hide	Arthur M. Budgett
1972	Roberto	Lester Piggott	Vincent O'Brien
1971	Mill Reef	Geoff Lewis	Ian Balding
1970	Nijinsky	Lester Piggott	Vincent O'Brien
1969	Blakeney	Ernie Johnson	Arthur M. Budgett

1968	Sir Ivor	Lester Piggott	Vincent O'Brien
1967	Royal Palace	George Moore	Noel Murless
1966	Charlottown	Scobie Breasley	Gordon Smyth
1965	Sea Bird II	Pat Glennon	Etienne Pollet
1964	Santa Claus	Scobie Breasley	Mick Rogers
1963	Relko	Yves Saint-Martin	François Mathet
1962	Larkspur	Neville Sellwood	Vincent O'Brien
1961	Psidium	Roger Poincelet	Harry Wragg
1960	St Paddy	Lester Piggott	Noel Murless
1959	Parthia	Harry Carr	Cecil Boyd-Rochfort
1958	Hard Ridden	Charlie Smirke	Mick Rogers
1957	Crepello	Lester Piggott	Noel Murless
1956	Lavandin	Rae Johnstone	Alec Head
1955	Phil Drake	Freddie Palmer	François Mathet
1954	Never Say Die	Lester Piggott	Joe Lawson
1953	Pinza	Sir Gordon Richards	Norman Bertie
1952	Tulyar	Charlie Smirke	Marcus Marsh
1951	Arctic Prince	Chuck Spares	Willie Stephenson
1950	Galcador	Rae Johnstone	Charles Semblat
1949	Nimbus	Charlie Elliott	George Colling
1948	My Love	Rae Johnstone	Richard Carver
1947	Pearl Diver	George Bridgland	Percy Carter
1946	Airborne	Tommy Lowrey	Dick Perryman

NOT WORTH A BET

In 1894 Ladas, ridden by Jack Watts, won the Derby priced at 2-9, and remains the shortest-priced winner in the race's history. Shergar, winner in 1981, is the most recent odds-on winner. The most recent odds-on loser was Entrepreneur in 1997, finishing fourth priced at 4-6 behind Benny The Dip.

THE MASTERS OF THE GOLD CUP

Pat Taaffe has won more Cheltenham Gold Cups than any other jockey in the history of National Hunt's most prestigious race. Taaffe guided the legendary Arkle to his three consecutive Gold Cup victories 1964–66 and then two years later partnered Fort Leney to success. Tom Dreaper has trained more Cheltenham Gold Cup winners – five – than any other trainer. Dreaper was responsible for all four of Taaffe's successes as well as winning the Gold Cup with Prince Regent in 1946.

BOMB SCARE NATIONAL WINNER

A few hours before the 1997 Grand National, the 150th running of the race, Merseyside police received two coded telephone messages informing them that a bomb had been planted at Aintree Racecourse. The bomb threats were reportedly from the Provisional Irish Republican Army. The police immediately evacuated Aintree with some 60,000 racegoers forced to abandon their vehicles in order that the police could carry out an extensive search of the area. Many of the jockeys, still wearing their silks, had to rely on the hospitality of local residents to feed them and provide them with somewhere to sleep until the following Monday when the rearranged race was run. BBC TV presenter Des Lynam was asked to leave the course during the live transmission. The race was won by Lord Gyllene ridden by Tony Dobbin and trained by Steve Brookshaw. Organizers allowed the general public to see the rearranged race for free.

UNIQUE GUINEAS DOUBLE

In 1809 Bill Clift rode Wizard, trained by Tom Perren, to victory in the inaugural 2000 Guineas. Five years later, the same jockey and trainer pairing won the inaugural 1000 Guineas with Charlotte.

RACING JARGON (9)

On the bridle – a term used to describe a horse that is running well, with plenty of energy left, and from which the jockey has not attempted to exert the maximum effort (also referred to as "on the steel").

AGAINST THE ODDS

Vespa (1833) and Jet Ski Lady (1991) are the longest-priced winners of the Oaks, at 50-1. Meanwhile, the shortest-odds winner was Pretty Polly in 1904, who crossed the winning line priced at 8-100.

IN HONOUR OF SCOBIE

Scobie Breasley, a four-time English Classic winner who always raced with a stopwatch in one hand, remains one of the most revered figures in the history of Australian flat racing. The annual medal presented to the best jockey in Victoria is named in honour of him, Damien Oliver winning the inaugural medal in 1996.

WILLIE CARSON, OBE

William Fisher Hunter Carson was born on 16 November 1942 in Stirling, Scotland. Although all he ever wanted was to be a jockey, it took a while for him to get established in the sport that was basically dominated by two jockeys at the time, Gordon Richards and Lester Piggott, both his seniors. In 1957 (the same year Piggott won his first Derby) Willie began his jockey apprenticeship with Captain Gerald Armstrong at his stables at Thorngill, North Yorkshire. However, it was not until 19 July 1962 that Willie managed his first win in the saddle, on Pinker's Pond, in a 7-furlong apprentice handicap at Catterick Bridge. For many years before landing his first Classic Willie actually contemplated quitting racing. However, the little Scot's drive and ambition to succeed won through in the end. In 1972 he landed his first Classic, the 2000 Guineas, riding High Top. In 1977 he rode Dunfermline, trained by Major Dick Hern and owned by Queen Elizabeth II to double Classic glory, the Oaks and the St Leger.

Willie was crowned Champion Jockey five times (1972, 1973, 1978, 1980 and 1983) and won 17 English Classics. He passed 100 winners in a season on 23 occasions, for a career total of 3,828 wins, thereby making him the fourth most successful jockey ever in Great Britain. His most successful season in the saddle was 1990 when he rode 187 winners, including six wins on a racecard at Newcastle in June – only three other jockeys achieved this feat during the 20th century. However, despite this massive haul of victories he only managed to finish second in the Jockeys' Championship that year to Pat Eddery who landed an amazing 209 winners.

In 1980 he took over the Minster House Stud at Ampney Crucis near Cirencester. Willie and his wife Elaine developed it into a state-of-the-art stud complex. In 1983 Willie was awarded the OBE in recognition of his services to horse racing. From 1982–83 he joined the former England rugby union captain Bill Beaumont as a resident team captain on the popular BBC TV series *A Question of Sport*. Willie retired from riding in 1996 aged 54. He was chairman of Swindon Town FC from 2001 until August 2007, and today Willie can be seen by millions of viewers alongside Claire Balding presenting coverage of racing on BBC TV.

Did You Know That?

Willie Carson was the only jockey in the 20th century to ride a horse to glory in an English Classic that he also bred – Minster Son in the 1988 St Leger.

DESERT ORCHID

Desert Orchid made an inauspicious start to his racing career. The grey, affectionately known as "Dessie", fell heavily in a novice hurdle race at Kempton Park in early 1983 and took so long to get back to his feet that the few in attendance that afternoon feared that his first race might also be his last. Thankfully Desert Orchid was unhurt and began the following racing season, 1983–84, on a winning note when he claimed victory in a novice hurdle at Ascot. In all, he won six times from eight starts in his first full season, but was unplaced behind Dawn Run in the 1984 Champion Hurdle at Cheltenham.

Having lost his novice tag, Dessie struggled against older. more experienced rivals in 1984–85, winning once in eight starts, at Sandown Park in February. His season ended in disappointing fashion, being pulled-up in both Cheltenham's Champion Hurdle and the Welsh Champion Hurdle at Chepstow and, in his final race of the campaign, he fell at Ascot. For the 1985–86 season David Elsworth switched Desert Orchid to chasing and immediately his winning form returned as he notched up four wins, at Devon & Exeter, Sandown and Ascot (twice).

On Boxing Day 1986 he romped home 15 lengths clear of Door Latch in the King George VI Chase. Dessie, who started at 16-1, beat horses of the highest quality, such as Combs Ditch, Forgive 'N' Forget and Wayward Lad. The 1986 King George VI Chase was Dessie's first win with Simon Sherwood in the saddle. Desert Orchid went on to win at Sandown and Wincanton. Then, in 1987–88, he won the Martell Cup at Aintree, his first win on a left-handed track, and the Whitbread Gold Cup at Sandown.

Dessie's greatest triumph came at Cheltenham in the 1989 Gold Cup, when 58,000 punters watched in the pouring rain as he overhauled Yahoo on a muddy track during the closing stages of the race to win by 1½ lengths. Speaking after the Gold Cup win his jockey, Sherwood, said: "I've never known a horse so brave. He hated every step of the way in the ground and dug as deep as he could possibly go." So heroic were Desert Orchid's efforts that the race was voted the best horse race ever by readers of the *Racing Post*. In 1990 Desert Orchid won the Irish Grand National.

Desert Orchid died on 13 November 2006. A statue of Dessie was unveiled at Kempton, where his ashes were scattered, a month later.

Did You Know That?
Desert Orchid is the only horse to have won the King George VI Chase four times – in 1986, 1988, 1989 and 1990.

SUNSTAR WINS IN THE RAIN

At the 1911 Derby a violent storm struck Epsom Downs which resulted in 62 millimetres ($2^1/_2$ inches) of rain falling in the space of only 30 minutes. When the rain abated the appropriately named Sunstar, ridden by George Stem, claimed the glory.

FLYING MACHINES ON FOUR SHOES

A thoroughbred racehorse is capable of going from 0 to 42 miles per hour in just six strides, a mere 2.5 seconds. Flat racehorses can reach speeds of up to 45 miles per hour, while steeplechasers can maintain a gallop of between 30 and 40 miles per hour.

RACING SCANDALS (4)

In September 1998, amateur jockey Angel Jacobs was discovered to be an ex-professional called Angel Monserrate. He had previously been banned for drug-taking in the USA and was exposed after riding in New York as an amateur under the name "Carlos Castro". The Jockey Club handed Jacobs a 10-year worldwide ban.

AGAINST ALL ODDS

The longest winning odds for a winner of the Grand National are 100-1, with four victorious horses having been returned winners at that price: Tipperary Tim (1928), Gregalach (1929), Caughoo (1947) and Foinavon (1967).

Three 100-1 shots have been placed since 1980: Over The Deel was third in 1995; Camelot Knight was also third in 1997, and Philson Run finished fourth in 2007.

WHEN FRANCE RULED ENGLAND

In 1950 France dominated the English Classics, winning all but the 2000 Guineas.

Race	*Winner*	*Jockey*	*Trainer*	*Owner*
1000 Guineas	Camaree	Rae Johnstone	Alexandre Lieux	Jean Ternynck
2000 Guineas	Palestine	Charlie Smirke	Marcus Marsh	HH Aga Khan III
Oaks	Asmena	Rae Johnstone	Charles Semblat	Marcel Boussac
Derby	Galcador	Rae Johnstone	Charles Semblat	Marcel Boussac
St Leger	Scratch	Rae Johnstone	Charles Semblat	Marcel Boussac

FROM THE HORSE'S MOUTH (6)

"We had no mobile phones then [to book rides], and we had no agents, we had to look for our own rides. We had to go and ride out and work in the yards. That's how it's changed."
***Jonjo O'Neill**, talking about the lives of the jockeys of his generation*

ALL EYES ON THE DERBY

The first Derby to be broadcast by the BBC took place in 1927 and was won by Call Boy (ridden by Charlie Elliott).

JUMPING A STONE WALL

In the early Grand Nationals the fences were usually just small country banks while some of them had ditches or a brook. Indeed, one of the early fences was actually a stone wall that was eventually replaced with the Water Jump in 1844.

RACING JARGON (10)

Off the bridle – a term used to describe a horse that is being pushed very hard by its jockey.

FIVE STANDS

Aintree has five main grandstands: Queen Mother Stand, Princess Royal Stand, County Stand, Earl of Derby Stand and Lord Sefton Stand.

AGA KHAN PULLS OUT OF BRITAIN

In November 1990, HH The Aga Khan removed all 90 of his racehorses from Britain. He shipped 30 to Ireland and 60 to France. This followed a row with the Jockey Club about drug-testing procedures when his 1989 Oaks winner, Aliysa, was disqualified after testing positive for a banned substance – Snow Bride was declared the winner some 18 months after the race. The Jockey Club alleged that a camphor derivative had been found in the filly's system but a furious Aga Khan said, "You're supposed to be innocent until proven guilty. But even if you're innocent, you have trouble escaping the image. The damage doesn't stop; it continues." However, in 1995 he renewed his association with British racing when he sent some of his horses to Luca Cumani's yard.

LADY FROM KENTUCKY

The 1904 Kentucky Derby was won by Elwood, the first Kentucky Derby starter and winner to be owned by a woman, Laska Durnell.

SEB TASTES FIRST OAKS SUCCESS

The 2008 Oaks was won by the 33-1 chance Look Here. Her victory gave trainer Ralph Beckett and jockey Seb Sanders their first victory in the Classic. Look Here's only previous start of the season saw her finish second in the Lingfield Oaks trial with Sanders, joint Champion Jockey with Jamie Spencer in 2007, in the saddle. "I made a hash of it in the Oaks trial but it was a trial and I found out a lot about her and it benefited us here," said a delighted Sanders.

NIJINSKY'S TRIPLE CROWN

In 1970 Nijinsky, owned by Mr C.W. Engelhard, trained in Ireland by Vincent O'Brien and ridden by Lester Piggott, became the 15th and last ever horse to win English flat racing's coveted Triple Crown. In the 2000 Guineas, he went off at 4-7 and beat Yellow God and Roi Soleil into second and third places respectively. In the Derby, the 11-8 shot came home in front of Gyr and Stintino. Then, in the St Leger, the prohibitively priced 2-7 favourite left the closest challengers, Meadowville and Politico, in his wake.

IRELAND'S 27 RACECOURSES

With 27 racecourses in Ireland (the North and the Republic), there are more courses per head of population than anywhere else in the world:

Ballinrobe	Bellewstown	Clonmel	Cork Mallow
The Curragh	Down Royal	Downpatrick	**Dundalk**
Fairyhouse	Galway	Gowran Park	*Kilbeggan*
Killarney	**Laytown**	Leopardstown	Limerick
Listowel	Naas	Navan	Punchestown
Roscommon	Sligo	Thurles	Tipperary
Tralee	Tramore	Wexford	

Bold = Flat only; *Italics = jumps only*. The others are dual purpose.

GIRL ON TOP

Fillies rarely run in the 2000 Guineas, normally opting for the 1000 Guineas. The last filly to win the race was Garden Path in 1944.

RACING ON THE SILVER SCREEN

Over the years many movies have been made about horse racing including the following:

The Big Race 1934 • *Bite the Bullet* 1975 • *Black Gold* 1947 • *The Black Stallion* 1979 • *Blonde Pickup* 1955 • *Blue Grass of Kentucky* 1950 • *Born to the Saddle* 1953 • *Champions* 1983 • *The Champ* 1931 • *Charlie* Chan *at the Racetrack* 1936 • *A Day at the Races* 1937 • *The Day the Bookies Wept* 1939 • *Dead Cert* 1974 • *Dick Francis: Blood Sport* 1989 • *Dick Francis: In the Frame* 1989 • *Dick Francis: Twice Shy* 1989 • *Don't Bet on Love* 1933 • *Down the Stretch* 1936 • *The Fighting Chance* 1955 • *Fighting Thoroughbreds* 1939 • *Four Against Fate* 1952 • *The Frame-up* 1937 • *From Hell to Heaven* 1933 • *The Galloping Major* 1951 • *Glory* 1955 • *Gypsy Colt* 1954 • *The Heist* 1989 • *Home on the Range* 1935 • *Horse Player* 1991 • *The Hottentot* 1929 • *Into the Straight* 1950 • *It Ain't Hay* 1943 • *Kentucky* 1938 • *Kentucky Blue Streak* 1935 • *King of the Turf* 1939 • *The Lady's From Kentucky* 1939 • *The Long Shot* 1939 • *Million Dollar Legs* 1939 • *National Velvet* 1944 • *Off and Running* 1991 • *On the Right Track* 1981 • *Phar Lap* 1983 • *The Rainbow Jacket* 1954 • *The Red Stallion* 1947 • *Run for the Roses* 1978 • *Saratoga* 1937 • *Shergar* 1999 • *Seabiscuit* 2003 • *Song of Kentucky* 1929 • *Sport of Kings* 1947 • *The Story of Seabiscuit* 1949 • *Sweepstakes* 1931 • *The Thoroughbred* 1930 • *Tip on a Dead Jockey* 1957 • *The Winner's Circle* 1948

Did You Know That?
Aldaniti appeared as himself in *Champions*. Bob Champion, played by John Hurt, was a consultant on the movie, but John Burke – a National winner on Rag Trade in 1976 – rode in the racing sequences.

EIGHT JUMP JOCKEYS IN 1,000-WIN CLUB

On 19 April 2003 Richard Johnson became only the eighth jump jockey to ride 1,000 winners. The 25-year-old claimed his 1,000th win when he rode Quedex to victory at Stratford. Johnson thought he had reached the landmark four days earlier at Exeter when he passed the winning post first aboard Mrs Philip, but after a stewards' enquiry, it was ruled that his horse had caused interference and they demoted him to second place.

Stan Mellor was the first to reach the 1,000 figure in December 1971, followed by John Francome, Peter Scudamore, Richard Dunwoody, Tony McCoy, Peter Niven and Adrian Maguire.

FOUR GREY DAYS AT EPSOM

Only four greys have ever won the Derby – Gustavus in 1821, Tagalie in 1912, Mahmoud in 1936 and Airborne in 1946. Terimon (second in 1989) and Silver Patriarch (second in 1997) were the last greys to be placed in the Classic.

AN EARLY START

At the 1951 Grand National starter Leslie Firth pressed the lever to release the starting tape with half the runners still milling around. However, the race organizers did not order a recall, leaving the stranded jockeys desperately attempting to get their mounts to set off after the others. Mayhem ensued, with many horses colliding at the fences leaving the field down to just five runners at the end of the first circuit. The race was won by the mare Nickel Coin at 40-1, the last mare to win the National.

2000 GUINEAS LEADING OWNER

Sue Magnier is the most successful owner in the history of the 2000 Guineas (1809–date), with a total of six winners (including shared ownership) in the race: Entrepreneur (1997), King of Kings (1998), Rock of Gibraltar (2002), Footstepsinthesand (2005), George Washington (2006) and Henrythenavigator (2008).

STABLEMATES CHALLENGE

Ruby Walsh went into the 2008 Gold Cup at Cheltenham having already tasted victory earlier in the day with wins on Fiveforthree and Celestial Halo. The Gold Cup finally paired stablemates Kauto Star and Denman in a much-anticipated first duel, with punters and racing commentators alike billing the race as the most exciting Gold Cup clash since Arkle beat Mill House in 1964. However, Walsh and Kauto Star were no match for Denman, winner of the SunAlliance Chase in 2007, who romped to victory in the showpiece race. Denman, the 9-4 second favourite and unbeaten in eight previous races during the season, won by 7 lengths with Sam Thomas in the saddle from the 10-11 favourite and defending champion Kauto Star. Neptune Collonges finished third with Mick Fitzgerald aboard, to land Paul Nicholls' Ditcheat Stables in Somerset a Gold Cup 1-2-3.

Walsh's only consolation after defeat on Kauto Star was that he won the Top Jockey Award at the Festival.

DERBY'S LEADING LADIES

In the history of the Derby ony six fillies have won the race:

- Eleanor (1801)
- Blink Bonny (1857)
- Shotover (1882)
- Signorinetta (1908)
- Tagalie (1912)
- Fifinella (1916)

RAF TRAINING COMES IN HANDY

In 1940 jockey Mervyn Jones was a flight sergeant in the RAF and with the Second World War just seven months old he had to seek permission from his air commodore to ride Bogskar in the Grand National. Legend has it that after Jones told his air commodore that he had recently passed his navigation exam, his superior said, "Go and navigate Bogskar around Aintree then, and if you don't, we'll put you through another navigation exam." Jones won the race on the 25-1 Bogskar. Sadly Flight Sergeant Jones was lost in action aged only 22.

CHAMPION FAILURES

Most National Hunt champion jockeys since 1960 have failed to ride a Grand National winner, including Tony McCoy (12 times champion), Peter Scudamore (8), John Francome (7), Stan Mellor (3), Terry Biddlecombe (3) and Jonjo O'Neill (2). Josh Gifford (4) did win a Grand National, but as a trainer, saddling Aldaniti in 1981.

2000 GUINEAS SHORTEST-PRICED WINNER

In 1896 St Frusquin, ridden by Tommy Loates, trained by Alfred Hayhoe and owned by Leopold de Rothschild, won the 2000 Guineas priced at 12-100 (around 1-8), the shortest-priced winner of the Classic since it was first run in 1809.

RACING JARGON (11)

Price – the odds that a bookmaker offers the punter to back a certain horse. If a horse wins at 10-1 the punter will get £10 for every £1 staked on the horse, therefore a bet of £1 on a 10-1 winner will win the punter £11 – his/her £1 stake plus £10 winnings.

♀

WHAT A FILLY

Sun Chariot, a daughter of Hyperion the 1933 Derby and St Leger winner, was owned by King George VI. Following an unbeaten two-year-old campaign, ridden by Gordon Richards and trained by Fred Darling, she won the 1942 1000 Guineas by 4 lengths. At the start of the Oaks, a few weeks later, she swerved to the left and lost a full 10 lengths to the leader before Richards kicked her into gear. She caught up with the field after a mile and then, a furlong from home, she hit the front and won by a length. After the race her jockey said, "It was one of the most amazing performances I have ever known." Sun Chariot's final race was the wartime St Leger, which she won in superb style by 3 lengths from the Derby winner, Watling Street, thereby landing the Fillies' Triple Crown for the reigning monarch.

DERBY–"KING GEORGE" DOUBLE

Only 13 horses have completed the double of the Derby and the King George VI and Queen Elizabeth Stakes in the same year.

Year	*Horse*	*Derby jockey*	*King George VI and Queen Elizabeth Stakes jockey*
1952	Tulyar	Charlie Smirke	Charlie Smirke
1953	Pinza	Sir Gordon Richards	Sir Gordon Richards
1970	Nijinsky	Lester Piggott	Lester Piggott
1971	Mill Reef	Geoff Lewis	Geoff Lewis
1975	Grundy	Pat Eddery	Pat Eddery
1977	The Minstrel	Lester Piggott	Lester Piggott
1979	Troy	Willie Carson	Willie Carson
1981	Shergar	Walter Swinburn	Walter Swinburn
1987	Reference Point	Steve Cauthen	Steve Cauthen
1989	Nashwan	Willie Carson	Willie Carson
1991	Generous	Alan Munro	Alan Munro
1995	Lammtarra	Walter Swinburn	Frankie Dettori
2001	Galileo	Michael Kinane	Michael Kinane

CHURCHILL'S WINNINGS

After he left the office of Prime Minister in 1945, Sir Winston Churchill became a keen racehorse owner and had a total of 27 winners. His most famous horse, Colonist (a grey), won 13 races to earn the former British PM £12,000.

ABC OF THE DERBY

When Quest For Fame ridden by Pat Eddery won the 1990 Derby it was the first time in the race's history that a horse beginning with the letter "Q" had won the Classic. It means that the only letters of the alphabet with which a Derby winner's name has not begun are now U, X and Z.

RUMMY THE NATIONAL HERO

After winning his record third Grand National in 1977 Red Rum became a national celebrity, opening supermarkets and annually leading the Grand National parade. His image graced many items from mugs to jigsaw puzzles, several books were written about him and many videos were produced showing his National victories. Rummy also helped open the "Steeplechase" ride at Blackpool Pleasure Beach in 1977 and appeared on that year's *BBC Sports Personality of the Year* show with his trainer Ginger McCain. When Rummy appeared before the selected audience of British sports stars at the BBC studios, Tommy Stack, who had ridden him to that third Grand National win, was in hospital with a broken pelvis. However, the presenter asked Tommy to say hello to Rummy via a live link up and amazingly, even though Rummy couldn't see Tommy, as soon as Tommy spoke Rummy's ears pricked up.

FREE FLIGHTS FOR THE WINNER

The budget Irish airline Ryanair said they would give away one million free flights on their website if their horse, Mossbank, won the 2008 Ryanair Chase at the Cheltenham Festival. Unfortunately for flyers, Mossbank finished second to Our Vic.

IN TRIBUTE TO GALILEO

Sixties Icon, the 6-5 pre-race favourite, swept to victory in the 2006 St Leger and was followed across the line by two blood relatives – The Last Drop, who finished second, and third-placed Red Rocks. Sixties Icon was sired by Galileo, winner of the 2001 English and Irish Derbies, who also sired the second- and third-placed finishers. The winner, trained by Jeremy Noseda for his owners Susan and Paul Roy, gave Frankie Dettori his second St Leger victory and his fourth win on that day's card. The horse was given his name to revive fond memories in his owner, Paul Roy.

LEADING SIRES IN BRITAIN AND IRELAND

The rating is based on the amount of flat racing prize money won by the sire's progeny during the season:

2008	Galileo	1986	Nijinsky	1967	Ribot
2007	Danehill	1985	Kris	1966	Charlottesville
2006	Danehill	1984	Northern Dancer	1965	Court Harwell
2005	Danehill	1983	Northern Dancer	1964	Chamossaire
2004	Sadler's Wells	1982	Be My Guest	1963	Ribot
2003	Sadler's Wells	1981	Great Nephew	1962	Never Say Die
2002	Sadler's Wells	1980	Pitcairn	1961	Aureole
2001	Sadler's Wells	1979	Petingo	1960	Aureole
2000	Sadler's Wells	1978	Mill Reef	1959	Petition
1999	Sadler's Wells	1977	Northern Dancer	1958	Mossborough
1998	Sadler's Wells	1976	Wolver Hollow	1957	Court Martial
1997	Sadler's Wells	1975	Great Nephew	1956	Court Martial
1996	Sadler's Wells	1974	Vaguely Noble	1955	Alycidon
1995	Sadler's Wells	1973	Vaguely Noble	1954	Hyperion
1994	Sadler's Wells	1972	Queen's Hussar	1953	Chanteur II
1993	Sadler's Wells	1971	Never Bend	1952	Tehran
1992	Sadler's Wells	1970	Northern Dancer	1951	Nasrullah
1991	Caerleon	1969	Crepello	1950	Fair Trial
1990	Sadler's Wells	1968	Ribot	1949	Nearco
1989	Blushing Groom			1948	Big Game
1988	Caerleon			1947	Nearco
1987	Mill Reef			1946	Hyperion
				1945	Hyperion

DETTORI'S HERO

Irish jockey Ray Cochrane won three English Classics in his career: the 1986 Oaks and 1000 Guineas with Midway Lady and the 1988 Derby on Kahyasi. He was presented with a Flat Jockey Special Recognition Lester Award and the Queen's Commendation for Bravery, both for saving the life of Frankie Dettori following a plane crash at Newmarket Racecourse on 1 June 2000. Cochrane – whose injuries in the crash led to his retirement – pulled Dettori from the burning wreckage seconds before it exploded, an accident that claimed the life of pilot Patrick Mackey. Dettori underwent surgery for a broken ankle and returned to the track just ten weeks later. "We went through hell and back together with the plane crash," said Dettori, who appointed Cochrane as his agent in November 2000.

FROM THE HORSE'S MOUTH (7)

"It is sad. I leave behind some great memories and certainly not from just the big days. I'm going to miss the weighing room very much – the lads are the best bunch of people you could ever wish to work with."
***Richard Dunwoody**, announcing his retirement in December 1999*

DERBY SUPPLEMENT

Kris Kin was entered for the 2003 Derby but was withdrawn at the end of the 2002 season. However, his owner, Saeed Suhail, had a change of heart a few days before the race and re-entered Kris Kin, paying the £90,000 supplement fee. It proved to be money well spent as the colt, trained by Sir Michael Stoute and ridden by Kieren Fallon, won. His victory gave Suhail the £852,600 winner's cheque. He was the first Derby winner to be supplemented for the race.

ONE FOR THE LADIES

The Oaks is now the feature of Epsom's Ladies Day and is run on the first Friday in June, the day before the Derby. It is the day when the ladies take centre stage both on and off the course.

RACING JARGON (12)

Each-way bet – when a punter backs a horse to win or be placed in a race. The each-way bet is two separate bets: one to win the race and one to be placed, so a bet placed at £5 each way will actually cost £10. To make a profit on an each-way gamble, a placed horse should go off at odds of 5-1 or greater, thus covering the winning half of the bet.

MOST NATIONAL APPEARANCES

Peter Scudamore's father, Michael, holds the 20th-century record for the most consecutive Grand National appearances with 16, including the winner in 1959, Oxo.

FLOCK TO CHELTENHAM

Almost 230,000 racegoers from across Britain and Ireland and further afield packed the stands on Prestbury Park for the 2008 Cheltenham Festival.

GRAND NATIONAL COURSE

1 & 17	A plain thorn fence standing 1.38m (4ft 7in) tall and measuring 83cm (2ft 9in) wide.
2 & 18	Similar to the first fence but 1.06m (3ft 6in) wide.
3 & 19	Westhead: open ditch standing 1.5m (5ft) tall with a 1.8m (6ft) ditch on the approach.
4 & 20	A plain fence 1.45m (4ft 10in) tall and 91cm (3ft) wide.
5 & 21	A spruce-dressed fence 1.5m (5ft) tall and 1.06m (3ft 6in) wide.
6 & 22	Becher's Brook: named in honour of the famous Captain Becher after he fell at the fence in 1839. It is one of the most thrilling and famous fences in horse racing measuring 2.03m (6ft 9in) on the landing side with a drop of 61cm (2ft) from take-off.
7 & 23	Foinavon Fence: a plain fence 1.36m (4ft 6in) tall and 91cm (3ft) wide. It is named after Foinavon, who was the only horse to jump the fence (as the 23rd) at the first attempt on his way to winning the 1967 National. It is the smallest fence on the course (excluding the Water).
8 & 24	The Canal Turn: a fence made from hawthorn stakes covered in spruce. It takes its name from the canal situated adjacent to it and horses take a sharp left turn on landing.
9 & 25	Valentine's Brook: thorn fence 1.5m (5ft) tall and 98cm (3ft 3in) wide with a brook on the landing side measuring 1.65m (5ft 6in) wide.
10 & 26	A plain thorn fence 1.5m (5ft) tall and 91cm (3ft) wide.
11 & 27	The Booth: open ditch 1.5m (5ft) tall and 91cm (3ft) wide, it has a 1.8m (6ft) wide ditch on the take-off side.
12 & 28	Westhead: a plain fence standing 1.5m (5ft) tall with a ditch on the landing side.
13 & 29	A plain fence 1.38m (4ft 7in) tall and 91cm (3ft) wide.
14 & 30	A plain fence 1.38m (4ft 7in) tall and 91cm (3ft) wide.
15	The Chair: with Becher's Brook, perhaps the most daunting jump in British horse racing. The tallest and broadest fence on the circuit at 1.58m (5ft 3in) high and wide, with a 1.8m (6ft) ditch on the take-off side. The ground on the landing side of The Chair is 15cm (6in) higher than the ground on the take-off side.
16	Water Jump: standing 83cm (2ft 9in) tall, this fence is the last fence on the first circuit of the National.
Run in	At around 450m (495 yards) long, many Nationals have been decided on this stamina-sapping run to the line.

FRANKIE DETTORI, MBE

Lanfranco "Frankie" Dettori was born on 15 December 1970 in Milan, Italy, the son of Gianfranco Dettori, a successful jockey and winner of the 2000 Guineas in 1975 and 1976. When he was eight, Frankie received a palomino pony from his father. In 1984 he left school to become a stable boy and apprentice jockey and moved to England a year later to become apprenticed to trainer Luca Cumani. In the winter of 1986–87 he rode 16 winners in Italy, the first being on Rif at Turin on 16 November 1986. Frankie's first English winner was Lizzie Hare at Goodwood on 9 June 1987. Cumani appointed Frankie as his stable jockey, replacing Ray Cochrane after Frankie became champion apprentice in 1989. He repaid Cumani's faith by riding 141 winners in 1990, becoming the first teenager to ride 100 winners since Lester Piggott, and he also won his first Group 1 race, on Markofdistinction in the Queen Elizabeth II Stakes at Ascot.

In 1991 he won 94 races in Britain, as well as the German Derby on Temporal, while in 1992 he claimed a second century of winners (101), and the French Derby on Polytain. It was around this time that Frankie adopted his low hands riding style, which reduces the pressure on the horse's mouth, thereby relaxing it. In 1993 he rode 149 winners to finish second in the Jockeys' Championship, but he won back-to-back titles in 1994 and 1995 with 233 and 216 wins.

Although in 1996 he rode "only" 123 winners, it included his "Magnificent Seven" at Ascot on 28 September 1996, the first time a jockey has ridden the winner of every race on a card in Britain. An accumulator bet – and there were many, especially on course – on Wall Street, Diffident, Decorated Hero, Mark of Esteem, Fatefully, Lochangel and Fujiyama Crest paid out at 25,091-1.

On 2 June 2000, Frankie and Ray Cochrane were aboard a Piper Seneca plane that crashed on take-off from Newmarket killing the pilot. Miraculously Frankie escaped with cuts and a broken ankle. He returned to racing barely two months after the incident.

Kazzia gave him his 100th Group 1 win in the 1000 Guineas in 2002 and in 2004 Frankie won his third Champion Jockey title (195 wins). Up until his win on Authorized in the 2007 Derby it was the only British Classic that Frankie had failed to win. The following day he won the French Derby on Lawman.

Did You Know That?

In 2000 Frankie Dettori bought Fujiyama Crest, the horse that completed his "Magnificent Seven", and immediately retired him to become a family pet at his home near Newmarket.

FROM THE FLAT TO THE JUMPS

In 1973 Sea Pigeon finished seventh in the Derby to Morston. The horse was then switched to jumps and went on to win the Champion Hurdle twice.

RED RUM'S IRISH HERITAGE

Rummy was bred in Ireland. When Maurice Kingsley, the first of Rummy's three owners, bought the horse in Dublin he paid 400 guineas for him.

2000 GUINEAS BIGGEST EVER FIELD

In 1930 Diolite, ridden by Freddie Fox, trained by Fred Templeman and owned by Sir Hugo Hirst, won from 28 runners, the highest ever entry for the Classic.

RACING'S GREATEST OF ALL TIME

In 2003 the *Racing Post* commissioned a poll from a panel comprising journalists, broadcasters, historians and racing administrators, to select who they considered to be the top 100 racing greats, excluding horses. Horse-racing pundit John McCririck made number 53 on the list! Here is the top 12 (figures in parentheses indicate the top three's share of the overall vote).

1. Vincent O'Brien (29%)
2. Lester Piggott (21.6%)
3. Sheikh Mohammed (12.3%)
4. Tony McCoy
5. Fred Archer
6. Martin Pipe
7. Sir Gordon Richards
8. Admiral Sir Henry Rous
9. Fred Winter
10. The Queen Mother
11. Phil Bull
12. Frankie Dettori

UNDER BALDING'S INFLUENCE

Ian Balding trained Mill Reef to win the 1971 Derby, ridden by Geoff Lewis. It helped Balding become British Champion Trainer that year. Among the many horses he trained was Lochsong, a bay filly/mare who won the Cartier Top Sprinter Award in both 1993 and 1994 and was voted the European Horse of the Year in 1993. In 1992 Lochsong won the rare sprint-handicap triple of Steward's Cup, Portland Handicap and Ayr Gold Cup.

2000 GUINEAS WINNERS 1946–2008

Year	*Winner*	*Jockey*	*Trainer*
2008	Henrythenavigator	Johnny Murtagh	Aidan O'Brien
2007	Cockney Rebel	Olivier Peslier	Geoff Huffer
2006	George Washington	Kieren Fallon	Aidan O'Brien
2005	Footstepsinthesand	Kieren Fallon	Aidan O'Brien
2004	Haafhd	Richard Hills	Barry Hills
2003	Refuse to Bend	Pat Smullen	Dermot Weld
2002	Rock of Gibraltar	Johnny Murtagh	Aidan O'Brien
2001	Golan	Kieren Fallon	Sir Michael Stoute
2000	King's Best	Kieren Fallon	Sir Michael Stoute
1999	Island Sands	Frankie Dettori	Saeed bin Suroor
1998	King of Kings	Michael Kinane	Aidan O'Brien
1997	Entrepreneur	Michael Kinane	Michael Stoute
1996	Mark of Esteem	Frankie Dettori	Saeed bin Suroor
1995	Pennekamp	Thierry Jarnet	André Fabre
1994	Mister Baileys	Jason Weaver	Mark Johnston
1993	Zafonic	Pat Eddery	André Fabre
1992	Rodrigo de Triano	Lester Piggott	Peter Chapple-Hyam
1991	Mystiko	Michael Roberts	Clive Brittain
1990	Tirol	Michael Kinane	Richard Hannon
1989	Nashwan	Willie Carson	Dick Hern
1988	Doyoun	Walter Swinburn	Michael Stoute
1987	Don't Forget Me	Willie Carson	Richard Hannon
1986	Dancing Brave	Greville Starkey	Guy Harwood
1985	Shadeed	Lester Piggott	Michael Stoute
1984	El Gran Senor	Pat Eddery	Vincent O'Brien
1983	Lomond	Pat Eddery	Vincent O'Brien
1982	Zino	Freddy Head	François Boutin
1981	To-Agori-Mou	Greville Starkey	Guy Harwood
1980*	Known Fact	Willie Carson	Jeremy Tree
1979	Tap on Wood	Steve Cauthen	Barry Hills
1978	Roland Gardens	Frankie Durr	Duncan Sasse
1977	Nebbiolo	Gabriel Curran	Kevin Prendergast
1976	Wollow	Gianfranco Dettori	Henry Cecil
1975	Bolkonski	Gianfranco Dettori	Henry Cecil
1974	Nonoalco	Yves Saint-Martin	François Boutin
1973	Mon Fils	Frankie Durr	Richard Hannon
1972	High Top	Willie Carson	Bernard van Cutsem
1971	Brigadier Gerard	Joe Mercer	Dick Hern
1970	Nijinsky	Lester Piggott	Vincent O'Brien
1969	Right Tack	Geoff Lewis	John Sutcliffe Jr

1968	Sir Ivor	Lester Piggott	Vincent O'Brien
1967	Royal Palace	George Moore	Noel Murless
1966	Kashmir II	Jimmy Lindley	Charles Bartholomew
1965	Niksar	Duncan Keith	Walter Nightingall
1964	Baldric II	Bill Pyers	Ernie Fellows
1963	Only For Life	Jimmy Lindley	Jeremy Tree
1962	Privy Councillor	Bill Rickaby	Tom Waugh
1961	Rockavon	Norman Stirk	George Boyd
1960	Martial	Ron Hutchinson	Paddy Prendergast
1959	Taboun	George Moore	Alec Head
1958	Pall Mall	Doug Smith	Cecil Boyd-Rochfort
1957	Crepello	Lester Piggott	Noel Murless
1956	Gilles de Retz	Frank Barlow	Mrs Johnson Houghton
1955	Our Babu	Doug Smith	Geoffrey Brooke
1954	Darius	Manny Mercer	Harry Wragg
1953	Nearula	Edgar Britt	Charles Elsey
1952	Thunderhead II	Roger Poincelet	Etienne Pollet
1951	Ki Ming	Scobie Breasley	Michael Beary
1950	Palestine	Charlie Smirke	Marcus Marsh
1949	Nimbus	Charlie Elliott	George Colling
1948	My Babu	Charlie Smirke	Sam Armstrong
1947	Tudor Minstrel	Gordon Richards	Fred Darling
1946	Happy Knight	Tommy Weston	Henri Jelliss

** Nureyev finished first in 1980 but was relegated to last place following a stewards' enquiry.*

RACING JARGON (13)

Running free – a term used (normally at the start of a race) to describe a horse that is going too fast to allow it to settle.

FIRST LADY OF KENTUCKY

The first woman to ride in the Kentucky Derby was Diane Crump in the 1970 renewal of the race.

PRIME MINISTER CHANGES NATIONAL

In 1947, at the request of Prime Minister Clement Atlee, the Grand National was run for the first time on a Saturday. The PM suggested the move in "in the interests of British industry". Caughoo, ridden by Eddie Dempsey and trained by Herbert McDowell, won at 100-1.

MILL REEF

Mill Reef was a small colt, foaled in 1968, owned and bred at Paul Mellon's Rokeby Stables in Virginia, USA. He was sired by Never Bend, the winner of the Eclipse Award for the Outstanding Two-Year-Old Male Horse in 1962, out of Milan Mill. An outstanding horse, Mill Reef won the Coventry Stakes, Gimcrack Stakes and Dewhurst Stakes in 1970, the Derby, Eclipse Stakes, King George VI and Queen Elizabeth Stakes and Prix de l'Arc de Triomphe in 1971 and the Prix Ganay and Coronation Cup in 1972.

Mr Mellon thought that his yearling's style better suited him to a career on Europe's turf courses rather than the more demanding dirt tracks of the USA so, in December 1969, he was shipped over to England to be trained by his young English trainer, Ian Balding, at Kingsclere Stables. Mill Reef made his debut in May 1970 in the Salisbury Stakes at Salisbury where he beat the 2-9 favourite Fireside Chat, ridden by Lester Piggott. He suffered the first of two defeats of his 14-race career in the 1970 Prix Robert Papin at Maison-Laffitte, France, to the very promising English colt My Swallow.

Mill Reef experienced his second defeat in spring 1971, being beaten by three lengths in the 2000 Guineas by another exceptional horse, Brigadier Gerard. However, cometh the hour, cometh the horse. His hour was the Derby, which he landed easily by two lengths from Linden Tree. A few weeks later Mill Reef captured the Eclipse Stakes at Sandown Park, beating the outstanding French colt Caro by four lengths. After his Sandown triumph Mill Reef, partnered by Geoff Lewis (his jockey in all of his starts), captured the King George VI and Queen Elizabeth Diamond Stakes at Ascot by six lengths from the Italian Derby winner Ortis. In October Mill Reef rounded off an extraordinary year by winning the Prix de l'Arc de Triomphe, beating the rising star of French racing, the filly Pistol Packer, by three lengths. This win at Longchamps meant that Mill Reef became the first horse to achieve the Eclipse Stakes, King George VI and Queen Elizabeth Diamond Stakes and Prix de l'Arc de Triomphe treble. After two wins early in 1972, he broke down and had to be retired.

Mill Reef ranked fourth on the list of Europe's Top 100 Horses of the 20th Century. He died in 1986 and was buried at the National Stud, where a statue stands in memory of this magnificent racehorse.

Did You Know That?

Mill Reef was given a rating of 141 by Timeform, the seventh highest rating ever given.

THE SUFFRAGETTE DERBY

In the 1913 Derby was perhaps the most dramatic of all time. Suffragette Emily Wilding Davison ran out in front of King George V's horse, Anmer, at Tattenham Corner and attempted to grab his reins. Davison, who joined the Women's Social and Political Union in 1906, had previously served several prison sentences including one for smashing windows at the House of Commons. The horse and his jockey, Herbert Jones, ploughed straight into her, resulting in Davison suffering a fractured skull. She was immediately taken to Epsom Cottage Hospital where she died four days later without ever regaining consciousness. Some spectators claimed that they heard Davison shout "Votes for women!", before climbing under the rail.

Queen Mary wrote to Jones, who made a full recovery, and in her letter said how sorry she was to learn of the accident that was caused by "the abominable behaviour of a brutal, lunatic woman".

RED MARAUDER

The 2001 Grand National saw only four horses finish the race, the winner Red Marauder, second-placed Smarty, Blowing Wind in third and the previous year's winner, Papillon. Red Marauder was ridden by Richard Guest and trained by Norman Mason. Guest's ride earned him the Lester Award in 2001 for Jump Rider of the Year. The trainer Martin Pipe had an incredible 10 of the 40 runners in the race, but only Blowing Wind, ridden by Tony McCoy, completed the course.

LANARK SILVER BELL

On 11 June 2008 Tifernati, ridden by Liam Jones and trained by William Haggas, won the Lanark Silver Bell at Hamilton Park. The Lanark Silver Bell is one of the world's oldest racing trophies. Some historians claim that it was first raced for 1,000 years ago, when it was gifted to Lanark by King William the Lion (King William I of Scotland). The 2008 race was the first time in more than 30 years that the trophy had been contested, the previous time being in 1977. Hamilton Park Racecourse won the right to host the 2008 Cash For Kids Lanark Silver Bell race in a public vote. Pop singers the MacDonald Brothers performed at the course, which was hosted to raise cash for charities in the South Lanarkshire and Glasgow areas. The £35,000 race replaced the annual Saints and Sinners race, which was transferred to Ayr after 42 years.

FROM THE HORSE'S MOUTH (8)

"The first time we all heard him [the starter] say false start. The second time nobody heard a thing. I did not know a thing until I saw people waving after I jumped the Chair."
***Peter Scudamore's** reaction after the void 1993 Grand National*

THE "IRON" DUKE OF ALBUQUERQUE

Many commentators consider the eccentric Spanish aristocrat, Beltran de Osorio y Diez de Rivera (the Iron Duke of Albuquerque), as the worst jockey in the long and illustrious history of horse racing. He became enthralled with the Grand National after he was given some film footage of the race as a gift on his eighth birthday. In total he entered the National seven times, with his first ride coming in 1952, when he fell at the sixth fence, almost breaking his neck. In 1963 he raced again, falling at the fourth fence, and in 1965 he fell again and suffered a broken leg when his horse landed on top of him. He fell at the 13th fence in the 1967 race and the general public was so mesmerized with him that the bookies offered odds of 66-1 on him completing a National.

The Iron Duke returned to Aintree in 1973 and fell off his mount after the eighth fence due to a broken stirrup. The following year he rode in a plaster cast after breaking his collarbone training for the race and this was after he had to have 16 screws removed from a leg he broke prior to the National. Amazingly he completed the 1974 National and finished eighth (last) on Nereo. It is claimed that the Iron Duke booked a private room in the Royal Liverpool Infirmary each year before riding in the National.

During a race in 1976 he was very seriously injured after falling from his horse and being trampled on by several other horses resulting in him ending up in a coma for two days. When he woke up he was told that he had broken a thigh bone, wrist and seven ribs, in addition to several fractured vertebrae. When he was discharged from hospital the 57-year-old announced that he would continue racing. However, the Jockey Club revoked his licence for his own wellbeing.

BRIT BREEDERS' BEST

Luca Cumani trained the only ever British winner of the Breeders' Cup Mile, Barathea in 1994, ridden by Frankie Dettori and owned by Sheikh Mohammed and Gerald W. Leigh.

ERIN GO BRAGH

In 1907 Orby, ridden by the American jockey John Reiff, trained by Dr Fred MacCabe and owned by Richard Croker, became the first Irish horse to win the Derby. Reiff's brother, Lester, won the 1901 Derby on Volodyovski.

OUTSIDER CLAIMS 2000 GUINEAS GLORY

The 66-1 rank outsider Rockavon, ridden by Norman Stirk, won the 2000 Guineas in 1961, the highest-priced winner ever in the Classic's history (1809–date).

LIGHT SHIFT AT EPSOM

Light Shift, ridden by Ted Durcan, gave trainer Henry Cecil an eighth Oaks victory in 2007. He now trails Robert Robson's record haul of 12 wins by four. Light Shift earlier won the Cheshire Oaks.

THE HORSE WHO LOVED CHEESE

Brown Jack, the legendary 1930s steeplechaser, enjoyed a devoted following of fans who regularly sent him his favourite food – cheese. In retirement he was immortalized in Philip Larkin's poem "At Grass".

POLEMARCH

In 1920, two-year-old Polemarch won the Gimcrack Stakes and Rous Plate. At three he won the St Leger, Great Northern Leger and Knowsley Dinner Stakes.

KATCHIT

Five-year-old gelding Katchit, trained by Alan King and ridden by Robert Thornton, saw off challenges from Osana and Punjabi to win the 2008 Champion Hurdle, the feature race on day one of the 2008 Cheltenham Festival. Katchit, who won the Triumph Hurdle at the same meeting in 2007, held off Osana by a length while Punjabi ran on to edge past the defending Champion Hurdler, Sublimity, to claim third place. A 10-1 shot, Katchit became the first Triumph Hurdle winner to win the following season's Champion Hurdle since Jimmy Uttley rode the Colin Davies-trained Persian War in 1969. The 2008 Champion Hurdle also saw a 1–2–3 for English trainers.

A GENIUS IN THE MAKING

Lester Piggott was only 18 years old when he won the Derby on the 33-1 shot Never Say Die in 1954, the youngest winning jockey in the 20th century. Piggott went on to ride in the Classic 36 times, winning an unparallelled nine times. Piggott's last victory was on Teenoso in 1983. In 1994 he partnered Khamaseen in his last ever Derby. The nine-times master finished fifth.

HORSE OF THE CENTURY FLOPS

In 1947 Tudor Minstrel, ridden by Gordon Richards, set the record for the biggest winning margin in the 2000 Guineas, romping home 7 lengths clear of the runner-up. However, the Fred Darling-trained horse, owned by John A. Dewart and hailed as "The Horse of the Century", was a complete flop in the Derby. He was the shortest-priced favourite for many years for the race and Richards was searching for that elusive win in the Classic. But he finished in fourth place and many punters blamed Richards for the horse's defeat, although Tudor Minstrel's subsequent races with other jockeys riding vindicated Richards as they too were beaten.

RACING JARGON (14)

National Hunt – the generic term applied to jump racing. The jump season runs throughout the year, ending with the Betfred Gold Cup Celebration Meeting at Sandown Park. The most prestigious meeting is the Cheltenham Festival, which takes place in March.

WILLIE'S IRISH DELIGHT

Willie Carson not only won 17 English Classics but he was also very successful in the Irish editions.

- Irish 1000 Guineas – Mehthaaf 1994, Matiya 1996
- Irish 2000 Guineas – Don't Forget Me 1987
- Irish Derby – Troy 1979, Salsabil 1990
- Irish Oaks – Dibidale 1974, Shoot A Line 1980, Swiftfoot 1982, Helen Street 1985
- Irish St Leger – Niniski 1979

Carson rode 3,828 winners and is the fourth most successful flat jockey of all time after Sir Gordon Richards, Lester Piggott and Pat Eddery.

SIR CHARLES FRANCIS NOEL MURLESS

Sir Charles Francis Noel Murless (known as Noel) was one of Britain's most successful trainers. He began his career as a trainer in 1935 at Hambleton Lodge in Yorkshire (where Kevin Ryan now has his stables) before moving to Hambleton House (where Bryan Smart now trains) shortly after the Second World War ended. In 1947 he was on the move again, this time to Beckhampton, Wiltshire, before moving for a third and final time to Warren Place, Newmarket, (where Henry Cecil now has his stables). He retired in 1976 and was knighted in 1977. In total he landed 19 English Classics, which included some notable doubles.

THE GOLD CUP NOVICE

The 1974 Cheltenham Gold Cup winner, Captain Christy, ridden by Bobby Beasley and trained by Pat Taaffe, remains the most recent novice to win the race..

RACING SCANDALS (5)

In 1982, a two-year-old colt named Flockton Grey won the Knighton Auction Stakes at Leicester by 20 lengths priced at 10-1. His owner, Ken Richardson, stood to make £36,000 while the bookies were set to lose £200,000. The horse won so convincingly that the bookies smelled a rat, and their suspicions were heightened when Flockton Grey disappeared straight after the race ended. The absence of the horse meant that a stewards' enquiry could not be held. Photographs were used in a subsequent investigation which concluded that the horse that won the race had been a "ringer". The police later discovered that Flockton Grey was actually a seasoned three-year-old horse named Good Hand, a horse also owned by Richardson, who claimed the mix-up was the fault of his trainer Stephen Wiles and that no wrongdoing had been pre-planned.

However, in 1984 Richardson appeared at York Crown Court with associate Colin Mathison and horsebox driver Peter Boddy facing charges of conspiring to defraud. Richardson was fined £20,000 and banned from UK racecourses for 25 years by the Jockey Club, while Boddy was given a 12-month conditional discharge and Mathison was handed a £3,000 fine. Twelve years later Richardson took his case to the Court of Appeal, claiming he was in possession of new evidence that would show his conviction was unsafe. However, his appeal was rejected and he was ordered to pay £50,000 costs.

THE LESTERS

The Lesters are the horse-racing industry's equivalent to the Oscars and recognize the outstanding achievements from both the flat and jumps. They were established by the Professional Jockeys Association in 1990 by the then chief executive, Michael Caulfield, and company secretary, Ann Saunders. The 18th annual Lesters awards ceremony was held on 20 March 2008. Each Lester awards category, apart from the Flat and Jump Ride of the Year awards, is decided on voting from the membership of the Professional Jockeys Association. Four nominations are made per category, with the Lester Award going to whoever receives the most votes. Tony McCoy won his 11th Jump Jockey of the Year Lester (1996–2004, 2006 and 2007) while Jamie Spencer claimed his second Racegoers Club Flat Jockey of the Year Lester, following his win in 2005.

2007 LESTER WINNERS

Flat Jockey of the Year .... Jamie Spencer
Jump Jockey of the Year .... Tony McCoy
Apprentice Jockey of the Year .... William Buick
Conditional Jockey of the Year .... Tom O'Brien
Lady Jockey of the Year .... Hayley Turner
International Jockey of the Year .... Ruby Walsh
Flat Jockey Special Recognition Award .... Kevin Darley
Jump Jockey Special Recognition Award .... Russ Garrity
Flat Ride of the Year .... Paul Hanagan – Fonthill Road, Paddypower.com Sprint Handicap, 13 October 2007
Jump Ride of the Year .... Andrew Thornton – Miko de Beauchene, Coral Welsh National, 27 December 2007

KENTUCKY DERBY LEGENDS

Only two jockeys, Eddie Arcaro and Bill Hartack, have ridden five Kentucky Derby winners. Arcaro also rode to two Triple Crown wins, the first on Whirlaway in 1941 and then in 1948 on Citation.

VICTORY ARC

The Prix de l'Arc de Triomphe, one of the French racing season's three Classic races, was inaugurated in 1920 when it was run in celebration of the Allies' victory in the First World War.

FOINAVON

The name of Foinavon is forever enshrined in the illustrious history of the Grand National with even a fence named after the winner of the 1967 National. However, the most remarkable thing about Foinavon, ridden by John Buckingham and trained by John Kempton, is not the fact that he is one of only four horses to land the National at the longest ever odds for a winner but the fact that he was an absolute no hoper who was well out of the race until carnage unfolded ahead of him at the fence that bears his name today.

Kempton, who was also his jockey, could not make the 10-stone weight Foinavon was assigned, so he gave Buckingham the ride and, thinking the horse had no chance of winning, went off to ride at Worcester. Foinavon was near the back of the field as the horses jumped Becher's Brook on the second circuit. However, when the horses approached the 23rd fence, one of the smallest on the course, some riderless horses – including Popham Down and Rutherfords – were leading the pack of those still racing. Popham Down got to the fence, swerved across the front of it and ran into Rutherfords.

The leading horses still in the race were distracted and refused to jump the fence, while more horses behind them stopped or swerved, with some hurtling their jockeys over the fence. Meanwhile, Foinavon was merrily trudging along at his own pace and when Buckingham saw the mêlée in front of him, he somehow guided his mount around the carnage and safely jumped the fence. Foinavon's lead at the 25th fence was about 200 yards, but it was down to 25 lengths as he claimed one of the most unlikely victories in the race's history. Foinavon returned to Aintree the following year to defend his crown but failed to make it past the Water Jump.

DERBY'S FIRST NON-EPSOM WINNER

In 1915 Pommern, ridden by Steve Donoghue, trained by Charles Peck and owned by Solly Joel, became the first horse to win the Derby away from Epsom when Newmarket staged the Classic during the First World War.

MAKE MINE A HENNESSY

Only one jockey has won the Hennessy Cognac Gold Cup three times – Willie Robinson. However, seven jockeys have two wins in the race: Graham Bradley, John Francome, Timmy Murphy, Paul Nicholls, Jamie Osborne, Peter Scudamore and Pat Taaffe.

FROM THE HORSE'S MOUTH (9)

"It was on my first morning as a 16-year-old apprentice at Fred Winter's yard. He'd asked me to muck a few horses out and I decided to take a radio down to keep myself entertained. When I turned it on the [horse] I was looking after bolted. Suddenly there were six loose horses charging around the yard."
***John Francome**, talking about the first time he got into trouble with a trainer*

STEVE NETS BOTH DERBIES

In 1985 Steve Cauthen became the first, and to date the only, jockey to ride the winner of the Kentucky Derby and the Epsom Derby. The American jockey rode Affirmed to glory at Churchill Downs en route to the US Triple Crown in 1978 when he was only 18 years old, and won the Epsom Classic for the first time on Slip Anchor in 1985. Cauthen was the first American-born jockey to partner the winner of the Derby since Frank O'Neill rode Spion Kop to glory in 1920. He won a second Derby in 1987 on Reference Point.

THE KING OF OZ

In 1926 William Watkinson became the first Australian to win the Grand National when he partnered Jack Horner to victory. Less than three weeks after his success Watkinson, from Tasmania, was killed at Bogside Racecourse in Scotland.

BLUE DITCH

Ffos Las (Blue Ditch), between Llanelli and Carmarthen, was on target for its June 2009 opening, the 61st racecourse in Britain and third in Wales. It will stage both jumps and flat meetings.

BACK-TO-BACK KENTUCKY DERBY WINS

Only four jockeys have managed to win back-to-back races in the Kentucky Derby – Issac Murphy (1890–91), Jimmy Winkfield (1901–02), Ron Turcotte (1972–73) and Eddie Delahoussaye (1982–83).

Bill Hartack narrowly missed out on back-to-back victories winning the race in 1960, 1962 and 1964, the last on the legendary Northern Dancer in a new course record time (2 minutes).

BOOKIES LEFT RED FACED

In 2001 William Hill bookmakers were ecstatic to finally get a version of their online bookmakers site up and running in China in time for the Grand National. The world's most prestigious steeplechase was being screened in China for the first time. However, unluckily for the British bookmaker, tradition and superstition play a huge part in Chinese beliefs, with their luckiest colour being, not surprisingly, red. And it was William Hill who was left red faced when all 2,000 new online Chinese gamblers bet on the 33-1 shot Red Marauder, who galloped home to victory.

LIKE FATHER, LIKE SON

In 2004 Ouija Board, ridden by the six-time Champion Jockey Kieren Fallon, romped to a 7-length victory in the Oaks. Ouija Board, sent off at 7-2 by the bookies, landed the filly's owner (the 19th Earl of Derby) and trainer Ed Dunlop a first English Classic winner. "We didn't know whether she would stay, but Kieren gave her a great ride, she got home well and won like a champion. I watched my father John train a Classic winner but to do it myself is amazing," said a delighted Ed.

Ed's father John won the 1000 Guineas three times, the Derby twice, the Oaks twice and the St Leger three times.

KEEP IT SHORT

Horse-racing regulations state that when an owner is registering a horse for racing, the animal's name may not contain more than 18 letters and/or spaces. Henrythenavigator has 17 letters in his name.

QUEEN MOTHER CHASE RECORDS

Most successful horse: Badsworth Boy –
three wins (1983, 1984, 1985)
Most successful jockey: Pat Taaffe –
five wins (1960, 1961, 1964, 1966, 1970)
Most successful trainer: Tom Dreaper –
six wins (1960, 1961, 1964, 1966, 1969, 1970)
Most successful owners:
George Ansley (1960, 1961, 1970),
Doug Armitage (1983, 1984, 1985) –
three wins each

1000 GUINEAS WINNERS 1946–2008

Year	*Winner*	*Jockey*	*Trainer*
2008	Natagora	Christophe Lemaire	Pascal Bary
2007	Finsceal Beo	Kevin Manning	Jim Bolger
2006	Speciosa	Michael Fenton	Pam Sly
2005	Virginia Waters	Kieren Fallon	Aidan O'Brien
2004	Attraction	Kevin Darley	Mark Johnston
2003	Russian Rhythm	Kieren Fallon	Sir Michael Stoute
2002	Kazzia	Frankie Dettori	Saeed bin Suroor
2001	Ameerat	Philip Robinson	Michael Jarvis
2000	Lahan	Richard Hills	John Gosden
1999	Wince	Kieren Fallon	Henry Cecil
1998	Cape Verdi	Frankie Dettori	Saeed bin Suroor
1997	Sleepytime	Kieren Fallon	Henry Cecil
1996	Bosra Sham	Pat Eddery	Henry Cecil
1995	Harayir	Richard Hills	Dick Hern
1994	Las Meninas	John Reid	Tommy Stack
1993	Sayyedati	Walter Swinburn	Clive Brittain
1992	Hatoof	Walter Swinburn	Criquette Head
1991	Shadayid	Willie Carson	John Dunlop
1990	Salsabil	Willie Carson	John Dunlop
1989	Musical Bliss	Walter Swinburn	Michael Stoute
1988	Ravinella	Gary W. Moore	Criquette Head
1987	Miesque	Freddy Head	François Boutin
1986	Midway Lady	Ray Cochrane	Ben Hanbury
1985	Oh So Sharp	Steve Cauthen	Henry Cecil
1984	Pebbles	Philip Robinson	Clive Brittain
1983	Ma Biche	Freddy Head	Criquette Head
1982	On the House	John Reid	Harry Wragg
1981	Fairy Footsteps	Lester Piggott	Henry Cecil
1980	Quick as Lightning	Brian Rouse	John Dunlop
1979	One in a Million	Joe Mercer	Henry Cecil
1978	Enstone Spark	Ernie Johnson	Barry Hills
1977	Mrs McArdy	Edward Hide	Mick Easterby
1976	Flying Water	Yves Saint-Martin	Angel Penna Sr
1975	Nocturnal Spree	Johnny Roe	Stuart Murless
1974	Highclere	Joe Mercer	Dick Hern
1973	Mysterious	Geoff Lewis	Noel Murless
1972	Waterloo	Edward Hide	Bill Watts
1971	Altesse Royale	Yves Saint-Martin	Noel Murless
1970	Humble Duty	Lester Piggott	Peter Walwyn
1969	Full Dress	Ron Hutchinson	Harry Wragg

1968	Caergwrle	Sandy Barclay	Noel Murless
1967	Fleet	George Moore	Noel Murless
1966	Glad Rags	Paul Cook	Vincent O'Brien
1965	Night Off	Bill Williamson	Walter Wharton
1964	Pourparler	Garnie Bougoure	Paddy Prendergast
1963	Hula Dancer	Roger Poincelet	Etienne Pollet
1962	Abermaid	Bill Williamson	Harry Wragg
1961	Sweet Solera	Bill Rickaby	Reginald Day
1960	Never Too Late II	Roger Poincelet	Etienne Pollet
1959	Petite Etoile	Doug Smith	Noel Murless
1958	Bella Paola	Serge Boullenger	François Mathet
1957	Rose Royale II	Charlie Smirke	Alec Head
1956	Honeylight	Edgar Britt	Charles Elsey
1955	Meld	Harry Carr	Cecil Boyd-Rochfort
1954	Festoon	Scobie Breasley	Noel Cannon
1953	Happy Laughter	Manny Mercer	Jack Jarvis
1952	Zabara	Ken Gethin	Vic Smyth
1951	Belle of All	Gordon Richards	Norman Bertie
1950	Camaree	Rae Johnstone	Alexandre Lieux
1949	Musidora	Edgar Britt	Charles Elsey
1948	Queenpot	Gordon Richards	Noel Murless
1947	Imprudence	Rae Johnstone	Jacques Lieux
1946	Hypericum	Doug Smith	Cecil Boyd-Rochfort

RACING JARGON (15)

Group/Grade 1, 2, 3 and Listed races – Group and Listed races are for the best flat racehorses. Grade and Listed races are their National Hunt equivalents. Group/Grade 1 races are the most valuable.

THE RACE THAT STOPS A NATION

The Melbourne Cup, Australia's most prestigious race, is dubbed "The Race That Stops a Nation". Run over 2 miles at Flemington Racecourse, Melbourne. on the first Tuesday in November, it is open to three-year-olds and over. Only 17 horses contested the inaugural Melbourne Cup in 1861, which had a purse of £170 and a gold watch for the winner. Archer won the first Melbourne Cup and retained it the following year. Efficient, the 2007 winner (trained by Graeme Rogerson, ridden by Michael Rodd and owned by Lloyd Williams) became the first horse since the great Phar Lap to win the Victoria Derby and the Melbourne Cup in consecutive years (1929–30).

PAT EDDERY

Horse racing is in Eddery's blood. Born Patrick James John Eddery on 18 March 1952 in County Kildare, Ireland, his father Jimmy won the Irish Derby in 1955 aboard Panslipper. Pat began his career as a jockey in 1967 and over the next three decades was one of the world's leading jockeys. In 1974, Eddery claimed the first of his Classic successes riding the Peter Walwyn-trained Polygamy to victory in the Oaks. The following season he rode Grundy to a Derby double, claiming both the Epsom and Irish versions of the Classic. However, perhaps his biggest breakthrough came in 1987 when a year after riding Prince Khalid Abdullah's Dancing Brave to glory in the King George VI and Queen Elizabeth Diamond Stakes and Prix de l'Arc de Triomphe, the Prince asked Eddery to be his retained jockey. Their partnership lasted until 1994 when Pat went freelance.

Many consider his victory in the 1986 Arc to be the greatest of his racing career. The field comprised no fewer than seven Group 1 winners but Eddery held his nerve, bided his time and released Dancing Brave at the right moment, a masterly example of the "waiting tactics" the brought rewards throughout his illustrious career. In 1985 he rode Pebbles to win the Breeders' Cup Turf and he landed the 1991 Breeders' Cup Sprint on Sheikh Albadou. In 1990 Eddery won the inaugural Lester Award for Flat Jockey of the Year, which he won again in 1991 and 1996, sharing it on the latter occasion with Frankie Dettori. At the end of the 2003 season Eddery decided to retire from riding and concentrate on becoming a trainer.

Eddery rode 4,632 British flat winners, a figure exceeded only by Sir Gordon Richards. When he rode more than 200 winners in 1990 he was the first jockey to reach the landmark figure since Richards achieved the feat in the year Eddery was born. He rode winners for many of Europe's leading owners and trainers. In terms of the greatest horses he has ever ridden to victory there are many to choose from – Grundy, Dancing Brave, Rainbow Quest, Danehill, Zafonic and Sadler's Wells to name just a few. Eddery was Champion Jockey 11 times – a record he shares with Lester Piggott – won the Epsom Derby three times (he has a total of 14 English Classic winners) and is the joint record holder for the most Arc wins with four.

In July 2005 Eddery obtained his training licence and established a stable near Aylesbury. His first win as a trainer came in April 2006 at Kempton Park with Visionist.

Did You Know That?
Pat Eddery was awarded an honorary OBE in 2005.

THE YOUNG AND THE OLD

The oldest winning jockey of the Derby was John Forth, who was in his 60s when he rode Frederick to glory in 1829. This victory also meant that he was the first man to ride and train the winner in the race. The youngest winning jockey of the Classic was John Parsons, who was 16 years old when he won on Caractacus in 1862.

IN MEMORY OF A LEGEND

The epitaph at the winning post of Aintree Racecourse where the legendary Red Rum is buried reads: "Respect this place, this hallowed ground, a legend here, his rest has found, his feet would fly, our spirits soar, he earned our love for evermore."

Did You Know That?
The comedian Lee Mack was Red Rum's stable boy.

FRENCH NATIONAL

The Grand Steeple-Chase de Paris is a Group 1 steeplechase in France that is open to five-year-old horses and above. The race is currently run in late May at Auteuil, Paris, over a distance of 3 miles, 5 furlongs, with 23 fences to be negotiated. The inaugural race in 1874 was won by Miss Hungerford. The 2008 winner, Princesse d'Anjou (winner in 2006 also), collected the majority of the winners' purse of 820,000 euros, making it the richest and most prestigious steeplechase in France. Only two horses have won the race on three occasions – Hyeres III (1964–66) and Katko (1988–90). Only 12 non-French-trained horses have won the race, Mandarin being the last to do so back in 1962. Two winners of the race have also won the Grand National – Jerry M and Troytown.

IRISH DERBY

The Irish Derby is a Group 1 flat race that is run at The Curragh, County Kildare, Republic of Ireland. The Irish Classic is open to three-year-old thoroughbred colts and fillies and is run over a distance of 1 mile, 4 furlongs, in late June or early July annually. The inaugural Irish Derby was run in 1866 and was won by Selim. It was not until 1962 that the race became a major fixture on the international calendar thanks to the increased prize money that year. The 1962 outing was the first under the title Irish Sweeps Derby.

NIJINSKY

Nijinsky was bred at E.P. Taylor's Windfields Farm in Ontario, Canada, in 1967. He was sired by Northern Dancer out of Flaming Page and his great grandsire was Nearco. The horse was named after the Russian ballet dancer of the same name because he had similar grace. In 1968 American diamond tycoon Charles Engelhard II purchased the yearling at Windfields Farm's annual auction for $84,000.

Engelhard shipped Nijinsky to Ireland to be trained by Vincent O'Brien at Ballydoyle Stables. Nijinsky inherited his sire's amazing turn of foot, an ability to move up through the gears like a Formula One racing car, and his mother's long legs (he measured 16 hands) and fiery temper. Indeed, he had such a temper he would very often refuse to canter, but O'Brien knew how to handle him and shaped him into one of the greatest racehorses the world has ever seen. As a two-year-old colt he comfortably won his first start in the Erle Maiden Stakes and went on to secure three of Ireland's biggest races for two-year-olds (the Railway Stakes, Beresford Stakes and Angeles Stakes). He ended 1969 by landing the Dewhurst Stakes at Newmarket.

Nijinsky was even better as a three-year-old, winning the English colts' Triple Crown, the first horse since Bahram in 1935 – and none has achieved this quite remarkable feat after him. He annihilated the field on his seasonal debut in Ireland's Gladness Stakes, making him the shortest priced favourite for the English 2000 Guineas since Colombo in 1934, at odds of 4-7. He won the race by 2½ lengths. On the eve of the Derby Nijinsky suffered a bout of colic that resulted in a blocked intestine, but he recovered in time to beat Gyr by 2½ lengths, going off at 11-8. Before he attempted the St Leger, Nijinsky claimed both the Irish Derby and the King George VI and Queen Elizabeth Stakes, his first run against older horses.

In late August, Nijinsky contracted ringworm, which severely hampered his preparation for the St Leger. Against O'Brien's wishes Engelhard entered him for the race, but he won by a length, his 11th consecutive win, a record for a British middle-distance racehorse. It proved to be his final victory because Sassafras was a shock winner by a head in front of Nijinsky in the Prix de l'Arc de Triomphe and then Lorenzaccio beat him in the Champion Stakes. In total, Nijinsky won 11 of his 13 lifetime starts, and he had career earnings of £436,000.

Did You Know That?
Nijinsky was retired to Claiborne Stud in Kentucky, USA, where, in 1986, he became the first stallion to sire Epsom and Kentucky Derby winners in the same year (Shahrastani and Ferdinand, respectively).

KAZZIA MISSES FILLIES' TREBLE

In 2002 Frankie Dettori claimed a Classic Double as the 100-30 favourite, Kazzia, trained by Saeed bin Suroor for Sheikh Mohammed, beat Quarter Moon by half a length to win the Oaks. Kazzia, winner of the 1000 Guineas (by a neck from Snowfire), became the first filly since Salsabil in 1990 to complete the Guineas-Oaks double. A foot abscess ruled her out of the St Leger thereby denying her the chance to land the coveted fillies' Triple Crown. Only two horses since the Second World War – Oh So Sharp in 1985 and Meld in 1955 – have achieved that treble. This was Dettori's third Oaks win; he had won on Balanchine in 1994 and Moonshell a year later.

RACING SCANDALS (6)

On 16 July 1953, Francasal won the Spa Selling Stakes at Bath priced at 10-1. However, a syndicate comprising of five men replaced Francasal in the race with a much better horse named Santa Amaro in an attempt to win an estimated £1 million from associated bets on the race. But their ruse was uncovered when it was discovered that a telephone line to Bath Racecourse had been cut to prevent news of large off-course bets being placed on the horse. The five conspirators were subsequently found guilty of fraud.

HOW TIMES HAVE CHANGED

In 1809 Christopher Wilson received 2000 guineas when his horse, Wizard, won the inaugural 2000 Guineas. When the silks of Sue Magnier's horse, Henrythenavigator, crossed the line first in the 2008 running of the Classic she collected a cool £212,887.50.

MICK CHANNON

When England international Mick Channon retired from football in 1986 he became an assistant trainer to John Baker and Ken Cunningham-Brown and four years later he obtained his own racing licence. His West Ilsley stable includes horses owned by the Manchester United manager Sir Alex Ferguson and his former England and Southampton team-mate, Kevin Keegan. Despite winning almost 1,500 races and £15million in prize money, he is still waiting for his first Classic winner. Sadly, on 27 August 2008 he was seriously injured in a one-car accident on the M1 motorway in Leicestershire which claimed the life of his friend Tim Corby, a bloodstock agent.

THE QUINTET

In the history of the Derby, two owners have had the distinction of owning five winners of the prestigious race. Lord Egremont's colours flashed past the winning post with Assassin (1782), Hannibal (1804), Cardinal Beaufort (1805), Election (1807) and Lapdog (1826). In the 20th century His Highness Sir Sultan Mohamed Shah, Aga Khan III, won with Blenheim (1929), Bahram (1935), Mahmoud (1936), My Love (1948) and Tulyar (1952).

BIGGEST EVER NATIONAL FIELD

The Grand National of 1929 witnessed the highest ever number of runners in the world's most famous steeplechase – 66. The 100-1 outsider Gregalach won the race.

RACING JARGON (16)

Odds-on – when the punter's potential winnings are smaller than the stake placed. Odds of 1-2 mean that if the horse wins the punter will get back £1 for every £2 bet, plus their stake. For example a £10 bet at 1-2 will win £5 plus the stake = £15.

RECORD BET

A record £300 million was bet by punters on the 2008 Grand National. Comply Or Die, the 7-1 joint favourite, won the race.

IN TRIBUTE TO LORD DERBY

Edward Smith Stanley, the 12th Earl of Derby (1752–1834), not only had the most famous Classic horse race in the world named after him, the Derby, but also the Oaks, which was first run a year earlier in 1779, is named after his luxurious home near Epsom.

FIRST TRIPLE CROWN WINNER

In 1853 West Australian, ridden by Frank Butler, trained by John Scott and owned by John Bowes, became the first horse in history to win the coveted English Triple Crown. When he was four years old West Australian won the Ascot Gold Cup, and after he was retired from racing he was sold as a stallion and latterly was purchased by Emperor Napoleon III in France.

ARKLE–MILL HOUSE DUELS

In the early 1960s two Irish-bred horses set the National Hunt world alight with their duels. In March 1963 Mill House, ridden by Willie Robinson and trained by Fulke Walwyn, won the Cheltenham Gold Cup and then the following November the pair teamed up again to land the Hennessy Cognac Gold Cup, with Arkle trailing him home in third place. Mill House's success made him the odds-on favourite to land the Cheltenham Gold Cup on 7 March 1964. During the showdown at Cheltenham, Mill House was scorching his way round the course with Arkle close behind. Then with three fences to go Arkle, ridden by Pat Taaffe and trained by Tom Dreaper, moved up the gears and raced away from Mill House to win the race by 5 lengths and set a new course record time. After the race a bewildered Fulke Walwyn said, "I can't believe that any horse could have done what Arkle did."

Arkle and Mill House renewed their rivalry in the 1964 Hennessy Cognac Gold Cup, with Arkle showing nothing but contempt for his opponent, winning the race by 10 lengths. Racegoers everywhere waited with eager anticipation for the 1965 Cheltenham Gold Cup and another showdown between the two Irish jumping legends. Arkle was imperious on the day, beating Mill House once again and this time doubling the winning margin over him to 20 lengths. When the pair met up once again at Sandown Park for the Gallagher Gold Cup on 6 November 1965 Arkle had to concede 16 pounds to Mill House. However, the additional burden had no affect whatsoever on Arkle who reined in Mill House's lead in the race before whizzing away to victory, again by 20 lengths. To rub more salt into Mill House's wounds Arkle bettered the course record by 10 seconds, a record previously held by Mill House.

Did You Know That?
Arkle was so far ahead of his rivals that handicapping rules were amended to give them a chance. When Stalbridge Colonist beat Arkle in the 1966 Hennessy Gold Cup, he was receiving 35 pounds

PADDY POWER FOR JOSH

Josh Gifford is the only man to have both ridden and trained the winner in the Paddy Power Gold Cup. In 1967 he rode Charlie Worcester to victory. He then trained Bradbury Star to back-to-back wins in the race in 1993 and 1994 (the race was known as the Mackeson Gold Cup from 1960 to 1995).

MONARCHS AND THE DERBY

In 1909 King Edward VII's horse Minoru (ridden by Herbert Jones and trained by Richard Marsh) followed up his success in the 2000 Guineas by winning the Derby, the only time the winner was owned by the reigning monarch (the King died the following year). He had also won the race with Persimmon in 1896 and Diamond Jubilee in 1900 when he was the Prince of Wales. King George IV won with Sir Thomas in 1788 when he was the Prince of Wales.

Queen Elizabeth II has won every Classic as an owner except the Derby. The closest she has come to winning was in her coronation year, 1953, when Aureole finished second to Pinza. Ironically, Pinza was ridden by the recently knighted Sir Gordon Richards, his first Derby win in 28 attempts.

GUINEAS PRIZE MONEY

The total prize money across all the races in the 2008 Guineas Festival was in excess of £1.15 million.

DERBY–ST LEGER DOUBLES

Since 1919, 11 horses have completed the Derby and St Leger double:

Year	*Horse*
1926	Coronach
1929	Trigo
1933	Hyperion
1934	Windsor Lad
1935	Bahram
1946	Airborne
1952	Tulyar
1954	Never Say Die
1960	St Paddy
1970	Nijinsky
1987	Reference Point

BON ACCORD

Bon Accord was second to Amicelli in the Christie's Foxhunter Chase at the 2008 Cheltenham Festival. Bon Accord was also the Scottish football team that suffered the heaviest ever defeat in competitive world football, a 36–0 Scottish Cup rout by Arbroath in 1885.

BETTING TAX AND BIRTH OF THE TOTE

In his spring budget of 1926 the Chancellor of the Exchequer, Winston Churchill (later Sir Winston Churchill and British Prime Minister), announced to the country in the House of Commons that a tax would be placed on horse racing in Britain with effect from 1 November 1926. Betting in Britain was legal at the time, but the Government's main aim was to curb the illegal betting that went on away from the racecourses on street corners. In a note to the Treasury he wrote that, "It would be essential to prohibit any notice, placard, list of betting odds or other street sign which would flaunt itself before the passer-by… Do not suppose that I have in the slightest degree made up my mind on this proposal, about which I entertain the gravest doubts," before adding, "I am afraid we might be accused… of having deliberately spread and multiplied the vice – I won't say vice, but evil?" Churchill estimated that a levy of 2–3 per cent on bets would generate income of around £3 million per annum for the Treasury.

However, this hugely unpopular tax proved difficult to implement with even the Home Secretary against it. Churchill found himself having to cut the tax rate twice before finally bowing to the pressure to repeal it. But he was not to be beaten and instead introduced a new scheme which did prove successful, the "Totalisator" (Tote), a machine which registered bets and gave the odds automatically. The Tote made its debut in July 1929 at Newmarket, under the control of the Racecourse Betting Control Board (RBCB) and was well received by the racegoers when it returned the winner of the opening race at 40-1 while the bookmakers' starting price for the winner had been 33-1. Bookies were suspicious of the new system at first and nicknamed the RBCB's wooden hut at Newmarket "The Hen Coop". But in the end Churchill's idea proved so popular with the entire racing fraternity that Lord Hamilton of Dalzell, a steward at the Jockey Club, wrote to him to thank him, "You have helped us to make racing a better and a straighter game than it has ever yet been and you have helped to prevent its becoming a game that only millionaires and sharps can play."

The Tote system is still used on British racecourses. Returns on winning bets (to a £1 stake, although the minimum on-course Tote bet is £2) are published after every race, along with the starting price. It is unusual for SP and Tote payouts to be identical. In 1966 the Tote introduced the Jackpot – where the punter has to pick the winner of six selected races – and the first ever winner took home more than £60,000 for a 5-shilling stake during the Royal Ascot meeting.

TRAINERS' 1–2

In 1948 Richard Carver became the first trainer to saddle the first two horses home in the Derby. My Love, ridden by Rae Johnstone, finished ahead of Royal Drake. Amazingly, it was the 64-year-old trainer's first ever visit to Epsom Downs. His feat was matched by Aidan O'Brien in 2002 when he saddled winner, High Chaparral, and runner-up Hawk Wing.

PARTY POLITICS

In 1992 Great Britain witnessed a general election and that year's Grand National was appropriately won by Party Politics, ridden by Carl Llewellyn and trained by Nick Gaselee.

RACING JARGON (17)

Trip – the distance of the race. Flat races are run over distances of 5 furlongs to 2 miles 6 furlongs, whereas jump races are usually run over distances of 2–3½ miles although the Grand National is run over a distance of 4½ miles at Aintree.

DUBAI MILLENNIUM

In 1999 Dubai Millennium was such a red-hot favourite for the Derby that most racing commentators thought all he had to do to win was turn up at Epsom Downs. However, the Godolphin-owned colt and His Highness Sheikh Mohammed's most favourite racehorse got himself so worked up before the race he was unable to regain his composure and could only sit back and watch Oath with Kieren Fallon in the saddle claim victory. His Derby flop (finishing ninth) was the only blemish on Dubai Millennium's impressive record: 10 wins from 11 races including the Queen Elizabeth II Stakes at Ascot and the Dubai World Cup in 2000 (setting a new course record at Nad Al Sheba of 1 minute 59.50 seconds).

His Timeform rating of 140, the highest in the world since Dancing Brave was awarded 141 in 1986, showed just how special he really was. However, in August 2000 his career was cut short by injury and he tragically died from grass sickness on 29 April 2001 before being able to fully prove himself at Sheikh Mohammed's Dalham Hall Stud. His one crop of offspring did produce Dubawi, who won the Group 1 National Stakes as a two-year-old and, aged three, won the Irish 2000 Guineas and Prix Jacques le Marois.

DON'T SCARE THE HORSES

Fearful of slipping standards, officials at Royal Ascot issued a clarification of the dress code for racegoers wishing to gain admittance into the Royal Enclosure in 2008. Women were instructed to eschew off-the-shoulder numbers, halter tops, spaghetti straps and micro mini skirts, midriffs were not to be bared and underwear not to be seen. Trousers suits would be permissible, but only if full length and in matching colours. Hats or "substantial fascinators" – feathery adornments – were to be obligatory. The fashion *faux pas* of fake tans, flashy jewellery and steepling stilettos were also warned against. Top hats, morning suits and waistcoats would remain mandatory for men (and no brown shoes). Stick to these guidelines and nobody would have to endure the social embarrassment of being turned away at the gate.

KENTUCKY DERBY AGE BARRIER

The Kentucky Derby is a race limited to three-year-old horses only, while no horse since Apollo in 1882 has ever landed the Derby without racing at age two.

BHA ORDER OF MERIT 2007–08

The British Horseracing Authority instituted a championship for jump racing for the 2004–05 season. Horses earn points for a top-four finish in 69 Grade 1, 2 and 3 races, with more points allocated for a Grade 1 race (20, 16, 12 and 10 points), than for a Grade 3 (10, 8, 6 and 5 points).

1. Kauto Star .... 100 pts
2. Lough Derg .... 94 pts
3. Voy Por Ustedes .... 79 pts
4. Our Vic .... 63 pts
5. Inglis Drever .... 60 pts

Kauto Star was crowned the winner of the 2007–08 Order of Merit after Lough Derg failed to make an impression in the Grade 2 Scottish Champion Hurdle. Lough Derg needed a top-four finish to wrest the crown away from the defending Order of Merit champion, but was ninth of 12 runners in the 2-mile race. Kauto Star's success gave his connections a nice £200,000 bonus, 75 per cent for his owner, Clive Smith, 12.5 per cent for trainer Paul Nicholls and 12.5 per cent for the stable staff at Ditcheat. Lough Derg won £75,000 for his connections.

RACING'S MOST FAMOUS YARD

No fewer than eight Derby winners have been trained at the Ballydoyle Yard located in County Tipperary, Ireland. Vincent O'Brien won six times, with Larkspur, Sir Ivor, Nijinsky, Roberto, The Minstrel and Golden Fleece, while the man he appointed to succeed him, Aidan O'Brien (no relation) won with High Chaparral and Galileo.

THE WAR HERO

The 1927 Grand National was the first to be broadcast on radio by the BBC. Meyrick Good and George Allison provided the inaugural commentary. The race was won by the 8-1 favourite Sprig, ridden and trained by Ted Leader. Sprig was bred by Captain Richard Pennington in 1917 during a period of leave away from the trenches in France. Pennington dreamt of riding his horse in the National after the war ended but was killed shortly before the end of the hostilities.

A VERY LUCKY PUNTER

Silver Birch, winner of the Grand National in 2007, helped one very lucky Irishman to a bumper payout of 500,000 euros. The unnamed married man bet his money on a four-horse accumulator and included the Grand National in his bet. He walked into a Paddy Power betting shop in Bantry, County Cork, a few hours before the Aintree meeting and placed his 20 (£15) bet on Silver Birch priced at 33-1 for the Grand National, 16-1 Kings Key and 12-1 Al Eile also at the Aintree meeting. When his first three romped home to victory he nonchalantly walked back to the bookies to watch his fourth and final horse, Paymaster General, win at 10-1 at Lingfield. The luck of the Irish!

SLIGHTLY FASTER THAN DETTORI

Frankie Dettori came third in the voting for the BBC Sports Personality of the Year award in 1996, the first jockey ever to be placed in the top three since the inception of the prestigious award in 1954. Damon Hill (Formula One World Champion) won the award while Steve Redgrave (Olympic rowing gold medalist) came second.

In 1970 the team behind the Triple Crown winner, Nijinsky, won the BBC Sports Personality of the Year team award.

BIRTH OF THE JOCKEY CLUB

The origins of modern thoroughbred horse racing date back to the 12th century, when English knights returned from the crusades with fast Arabian horses. The next 400 years saw a steady increase of Arabian stallions brought over to England to breed with English mares, with the nobility at the time issuing challenge races to other horse owners for an agreed wager. However, it wasn't until well into Queen Anne's reign (1702–14) that races involving a number of horses were staged whereby the spectators could place bets on the runners. The latter meetings spread throughout the country, resulting in a meeting of horse racing's elite at Newmarket in 1750, the outcome of which was the formation of the Jockey Club, which over 250 years later has complete control over English racing.

The Jockey Club drew up a complete set of rules to govern the sport and permitted racecourses to host race meetings under the rules. In addition to exercising control over the race meetings, the Jockey Club also issued rules governing the breeding of racehorses.

STEVE'S ST LEGER DOUBLE

In 1915 Steve Donoghue rode Pommern to victory in the St Leger for trainer Charley Peck and owner Solly Joel. Two years later Donoghue won the Classic again, his final win in the race, on Gay Crusader, trained by Alec Taylor Jr and owned by Alfred W. Cox.

A HUGE INDUSTRY

In 2008 the racing and breeding industry in Britain was responsible for almost 50,000 full-time employees while another 40,000 were employed in the betting industry. It has been estimated that 33 per cent of the jobs in Newmarket are directly related to horse racing and 66 per cent of bets placed in Britain are bet on horse racing.

NIJINSKY IS FIRST OF O'BRIEN'S SEVEN

Nijinsky's 1969 win in Newmarket's most prestigious two-year-olds' race, the Dewhurst Stakes, was significant in that it was the first of seven successes for the future Triple Crown winner's trainer, Vincent O'Brien. The legendary Irish trainer, regarded by many as the greatest trainer of the 20th century, also won with Cellini (1973), The Minstrel (1976), Try My Best (1977), Monteverdi (1979), Storm Bird (1980) and El Gran Senor (1983).

FROM THE HORSE'S MOUTH (10)

"Ninety per cent of riding horses is in your head. Physically, anybody can be taught to ride to a certain level. The hard part about riding is the racing brain. How fast we're going, where the best ground is, which is the right horse to be following, where the winning post is – there are tons of different calculations."
***Ruby Walsh**, 2007*

MASTER TRAINER

Vincent O'Brien is the only living person to have trained the winner of the Derby, the Cheltenham Gold Cup and the Grand National. Larkspur won the 1962 Derby, the first of his six winners, and he won the Grand National in three consecutive years with Early Mist in 1953, Royal Tan in 1954 and Quare Times in 1955. Cottage Rake won the Gold Cup in three consecutive years (1948–50) and Knock Hard gave O'Brien his fourth Gold Cup in 1953.

RACING JARGON (18)

Going – the term used to describe the condition of the ground on the course. In Britain, the going can be heavy, soft, good-to-soft, good, good-to-firm, firm and hard, with variances in places. On all-weather tracks the going is fast, slow or standard. If the going changes suddenly, horses can be withdrawn without penalty.

THE PSYCHIC JOCKEY

The 1952 Grand National had a 12-minute delay after the 47 runners prematurely charged the tape. Rumour has it that before the restart Teal's jockey Arthur Thompson said, "I thought I would have been in the winner's enclosure by now." About 15 minutes later they did enter the winner's enclosure in triumph, priced at 100-7.

LOVE IS IN THE AIR

Well, for five months of the year anyway. The breeding season starts on the day after St Valentine's Day (15 February) and lasts until 15 July. When a mare is in season her breeder will bring a "teaser" to her stable box. The teaser effectively arouses the mare and when she's in the mood the breeder removes the teaser and introduces the stallion. Be My Native once covered 325 mares in a single year.

THE CLASSICS

There are five "Classic" flat races in Britain. They are open to three-year-old horses only:

Classic	*Date*	*Distance*	*Racecourse*
2000 Guineas	Late April/early May	1 mile	Newmarket
1000 Guineas*	Late April/early May	1 mile	Newmarket
Oaks*	Early June	1m 4f 10y	Epsom
Derby	First Saturday in June	1m 4f 10y	Epsom
St Leger	September	1m 6f 132y	Doncaster

* *The 1000 Guineas and the Oaks are restricted to fillies only.*

SIR GORDON LEADS THE WAY

Sir Gordon Richards is the most prolific jockey in the history of British racing. The 26-time Champion Jockey rode 4,870 winners from his 21,843 races during his career, which spanned three decades. However, he trails the world's leading jockeys by a considerable margin. On 9 January 2008, Jorge Ricardo (Brazil, aged 46) became the first jockey to ride 10,000 winners, while Russell Baze (USA, aged 50) claimed his 10,000th winner just 22 days later. Baze won his first race in 1974; Ricardo landed his first in 1976.

YOUNG IRISHMAN FOLLOWS RICHARDS

In 1974, Pat Eddery, from County Kildare, Ireland, was crowned Champion Flat Jockey. At 22 years of age he was the youngest champion since 21-year-old Gordon Richards in 1925.

HAPPY BIRTHDAY

All Northern Hemisphere racehorses celebrate their birthdays on 1 January, which makes it easier to group them together in age groups for races. Consequently it is desirable to have racehorses foaled as soon after New Year's Day as possible in order that they will be more mature by the time they commence racing as two-year-olds.

FRESH TURF

Great Leighs Racecourse, located near Chelmsford in Essex, became Britain's first completely new racecourse for 80 years when it opened on 20 April 2008. Taunton had been the last new course to open.

TONY McCOY, MBE

Anthony Peter (Tony, or A.P. as he appears on racecards) McCoy was born on 4 May 1974 in Moneyglass, County Antrim, Northern Ireland. An obsessive sportsman, he is considered the greatest jump jockey of all time. When he was just 11 years old a local horse-trader named Billy Rock offered the young McCoy the opportunity to work at his yard and he jumped at the chance.

After four and a half happy years at the yard, Rock suggested that McCoy should take up a career as a jockey and arranged for him to see the flat-racing trainer, Jim Bolger, in Kilkenny. McCoy rode his first ever winner, Legal Steps, on 26 March 1992 at Thurles. However, within 10 months his racing career almost came to an end when he suffered a heavy fall while riding Kly Green on the gallops. He broke his leg and was out of action for five months. When he returned he rode 12 more winners for Bolger before joining Toby Balding's yard in England, and he switched to jump racing. His impact was immediate, winning a record 74 races and taking the conditional jockeys' title in his debut season, 1994–95.

The following season, McCoy landed the Jockeys' Championship, a feat that he has repeated in every season to date. His first major success came at the Cheltenham Festival in 1996 when he rode Kibreet to glory in the Grand Annual Chase. McCoy was then attached to Paul Nicholls' yard, but midway through the 1996–97 season he teamed up with Martin Pipe. After glorious years, McCoy was lured by Irish millionaire J.P. McManus to be his retained jockey, and since 2004 McCoy has often ridden for Jonjo O'Neill.

McCoy's has ridden more than 200 winners in six separate seasons and reached 1,000 wins in the shortest time. On 2 April 2002, McCoy passed Sir Gordon Richards' 55-year-old record for the most winners in a season for all types of racing with his 270th success, Valfonic, at Warwick. Amazingly he went on to land 289 winners in 2001–02, which remains a British record. Win number 289 on Mighty Manifesto saw him overtake Richard Dunwoody's record of all-time jumps winners. If he avoids serious injury, McCoy should celebrate his 3,000th winner sometime in 2009. But he has never landed the one victory he covets most – the Grand National.

Did You Know That?

Tony McCoy has a television in almost every room in his house, all showing racing channels. He even has a TV in the bathroom, which he watches while taking intensely hot baths as part of his strict weight-losing regime.

ONE AND ONLY

Jenny Pitman remains the only woman to have trained a Grand National winner (Corbiere in 1983 and Royal Athlete in 1995). The last of her 39 runners in the race, Nahthen Lad, finished eleventh in 1999.

THE ENGLISH TRIPLE CROWN

The English Triple Crown for three-year-olds comprises three Group 1 races – the 2000 Guineas, Derby and St Leger. In the history of English racing there have only ever been 15 Triple Crown winners and none since 1970:

1853 West Australian
1865 Gladiateur
1866 Lord Lyon
1886 Ormonde
1891 Common
1893 Isinglass
1897 Galtee More
1899 Flying Fox
1900 Diamond Jubilee
1903 Rock Sand
1915 Pommern
1917 Gay Crusader
1918 Gainsborough
1935 Bahram
1970 Nijinsky

RUNNER-UP TO SOCCER

In Britain horse racing is second only to football when measured by revenue and spectator numbers.

PIGGOTT BANNED

Following the 1954 King Edward VII Stakes at Royal Ascot, 19-year-old Lester Piggott was, in the opinion of many racegoers, wrongly blamed by the stewards for causing a jostling of horses early in the straight. Piggott was handed a six-month ban from Ascot by the Jockey Club, who also ordered him to continue his apprenticeship away from his father (a trainer at the time), who they thought was pushing him too far in his quest to succeed. Lester packed his bags and teamed up with Jack Jarvis in Newmarket.

SO MANY NEWBORNS

There are 5,000 thoroughbred racehorses foaled in Britain every year and 110,000 worldwide.

GRAND NATIONAL WINNERS 1946–2008

Year	*Winner*	*Jockey*	*Trainer*
2008	Comply or Die	Timmy Murphy	David Pipe
2007	Silver Birch	Robbie Power	Gordon Elliott
2006	Numbersixvalverde	Niall Madden	Martin Brassil
2005	Hedgehunter	Ruby Walsh	Willie Mullins
2004	Amberleigh House	Graham Lee	Ginger McCain
2003	Monty's Pass	Barry Geraghty	Jimmy Mangan
2002	Bindaree	Jim Culloty	Nigel Twiston-Davies
2001	Red Marauder	Richard Guest	Norman Mason
2000	Papillon	Ruby Walsh	Ted Walsh
1999	Bobbyjo	Paul Carberry	Tommy Carberry
1998	Earth Summit	Carl Llewellyn	Nigel Twiston-Davies
1997	Lord Gyllene	Tony Dobbin	Steve Brookshaw
1996	Rough Quest	Mick Fitzgerald	Terry Casey
1995	Royal Athlete	Jason Titley	Jenny Pitman
1994	Miinnehoma	Richard Dunwoody	Martin Pipe
1992	Party Politics	Carl Llewellyn	Nick Gaselee
1993*	*race void*		
1991	Seagram	Nigel Hawke	David Barons
1990	Mr Frisk	Mr Marcus Armytage	Kim Bailey
1989	Little Polveir	Jimmy Frost	Toby Balding
1988	Rhyme 'N' Reason	Brendan Powell	David Elsworth
1987	Maori Venture	Steve Knight	Andrew Turnell
1986	West Tip	Richard Dunwoody	Michael Oliver
1985	Last Suspect	Hywel Davies	Tim Forster
1984	Hallo Dandy	Neale Doughty	Gordon W. Richards
1983	Corbiere	Ben de Haan	Jenny Pitman
1982	Grittar	Mr Dick Saunders	Frank Gilman
1981	Aldaniti	Bob Champion	Josh Gifford
1980	Ben Nevis	Mr Charlie Fenwick	Tim Forster
1979	Rubstic	Maurice Barnes	John Leadbetter
1978	Lucius	Bob Davies	Gordon W. Richards
1977	Red Rum	Tommy Stack	Ginger McCain
1976	Rag Trade	John Burke	Fred Rimell
1975	L'Escargot	Tommy Carberry	Dan Moore
1974	Red Rum	Brian Fletcher	Ginger McCain
1973	Red Rum	Brian Fletcher	Ginger McCain
1972	Well To Do	Graham Thorner	Tim Forster
1971	Specify	John Cook	John Sutcliffe
1970	Gay Trip	Pat Taaffe	Fred Rimell
1969	Highland Wedding	Eddie Harty	Toby Balding

1968	Red Alligator	Brian Fletcher	Denys Smith
1967	Foinavon	John Buckingham	John Kempton
1966	Anglo	Tim Norman	Fred Winter
1965	Jay Trump	Mr Tommy Smith	Fred Winter
1964	Team Spirit	Willie Robinson	Fulke Walwyn
1963	Ayala	Pat Buckley	Keith Piggott
1962	Kilmore	Fred Winter	Ryan Price
1961	Nicolaus Silver	Bobby Beasley	Fred Rimell
1960	Merryman II	Gerry Scott	Neville Crump
1959	Oxo	Michael Scudamore	Willie Stephenson
1958	Mr What	Arthur Freeman	Tom Taaffe
1957	Sundew	Fred Winter	Frank Hudson
1956	E.S.B.	Dave Dick	Fred Rimell
1955	Quare Times	Pat Taaffe	Vincent O'Brien
1954	Royal Tan	Bryan Marshall	Vincent O'Brien
1953	Early Mist	Bryan Marshall	Vincent O'Brien
1952	Teal	Arthur Thompson	Neville Crump
1951	Nickel Coin	John Bullock	Jack O'Donoghue
1950	Freebooter	Jimmy Power	Bobby Renton
1949	Russian Hero	Leo McMorrow	George Owen
1948	Sheila's Cottage	Arthur Thompson	Neville Crump
1947	Caughoo	Eddie Dempsey	Herbert McDowell
1946	Lovely Cottage	Captain Bobby Petre	Tommy Rayson

* *The 1993 race was declared void after a false start. Esha Ness was first past the post.*

DERBY KINGS

Three trainers have trained a record seven Derby winners: Robert Robson, John Porter and Fred Darling. Among current or recent trainers, the most successful are Henry Cecil and Sir Michael Stoute with four. Cecil won with Slip Anchor (1985), Reference Point (1987), Commander In Chief (1993) and Oath (1999). Stoute's winners were: Shergar (1981), Shahrastani (1986), Kris Kin (2003) and North Light (2004). Kieren Fallon rode three of these winners: Oath, Kris Kin and North Light.

RACING JARGON (19)

Handicap – Each horse is rated according to its form in previous races and assigned a weight compared to other horses in the race – its handicap. The main purpose of the handicap system is to allow the lesser-rated horses in the race a better chance of winning.

PHAR LAP

This mighty chestnut, nicknamed "The Red Terror" and "Big Red", was foaled on 4 October 1926, sired by Night Raid out of Entreaty at Timaru, New Zealand. However, he never raced in New Zealand and was purchased for 160 guineas by Hugh Telford on behalf his brother Harry, a struggling trainer in Sydney, at the 1928 Trentham Yearling Sales. When Hugh Telford could not raise the funds for the fee he sold him on to the American sportsman David J. Davis.

Phar Lap arrived in Australia looking gangly (though he eventually grew to 17.1 hands) with an awkward gait and warts on his face. Davis was furious and refused to pay any training fees. As Davis was one of Harry Telford's few remaining owners, he agreed to train Phar Lap for free in return for two-thirds of any winnings. In his first outing he came in last and was unplaced in his next three races, all as a two-year-old. On 27 April 1929, aged three, he claimed his first victory, the Maiden Juvenile Handicap at Rosehill. Another four unplaced finishes followed before he took Australian racing by storm.

Over the next 2½ years he was the most dominant horse in Australia, winning 36 times in 41 starts. Phar Lap's first major victory came in the 1929 Rosehill Guineas, before easily landing the AJC Derby in a new course record time. Jim Pike rode Phar Lap and the pair proved a successful partnership, notching up 25 of Phar Lap's 37 wins. After winning the 1929 Victoria Derby Phar Lap was only third in the Melbourne Cup, then second in the St George's Stakes at Caulfield before claiming nine wins in a row.

After losing his first race as a four-year-old in spring 1930 Phar Lap went on an amazing run of 14 consecutive victories including the prestigious W.S. Cox Plate and the Melbourne Cup. He won the Cup by 3 lengths with a weight-carrying record of 9st 12lbs.

After winning five times as a five-year-old he was sent to America to try and win some big prize money and won his first race, the Agua Caliente Handicap, in a new course record time. However, 16 days later he fell ill and died. Over the years many scientists and veterinarians have put forward theories and findings as to the cause of death. In June 2008, Dr Ivan Kempson and Dermot Henry, from the Melbourne Museum. concluded that in the 30–40 hours prior to death, he had ingested a massive dose of arsenic. Phar Lap remains a much-loved Australian icon.

Did You Know That?
The name Phar Lap derives from the shared Thai and Zhuang word for lightning.

THE NATIONAL THAT NEVER WAS

The 1993 Aintree Grand National will always be remembered as "the race that never was". As the horses lined up at the tape some demonstrators could be seen further down the course, and so the starter Keith Brown told the jockeys to "take a turn" and walk back to the tape. As the jockeys pushed their mounts forward to the starting line a false start occurred when the starting tape failed to rise correctly and actually became entangled around some of the horses. Brown immediately raised the red flag to signify a false start and all of the horses pulled up before the first fence.

After the horses lined up again many of them were sweating profusely and acting up as the noise from the crowd became louder in anticipation of the race getting under way. However, a second false start occurred when the limp tape again failed to rise properly and actually was caught around Richard Dunwoody's throat. Brown produced his red flag again but apparently the recall assistant further down the course could not see it being waved and so 30 of the 39 jockeys who set off were completely unaware of the false start. Some of the course officials tried to stop the horses by waving red flags next to The Chair at the end of the first circuit, but those jockeys still riding thought the red flags were being waved by more protestors and continued racing. Indeed, Peter Scudamore only stopped racing because he saw his usual trainer Martin Pipe frantically waving at him.

Seven horses ran the full 4½ miles, with Esha Ness, ridden by John White and trained by Jenny Pitman, passing the winning post first. The stewards immediately held an inquiry and officially declared the 1993 Grand National void. When he was interviewed after the race John White said, "The first false start I saw a chap with a white flag I knew I had not gone 20 yards and I pulled up knowing it was a false start. When we jumped off the second time, I have not seen a rerun of the race I was up there with the first half dozen I didn't see any flag." The following year the starting tapes were changed and instead of the tapes going up vertically they were made to rise at a 45-degree angle away from the horses.

CHELTENHAM GOLD CUP LUCKY TOUCH

Dorothy Paget holds the record for the most Cheltenham Gold Cup wins by any owner, an astonishing seven. Five of her wins came courtesy of the legendary Golden Miller who won the race for five consecutive years (1932–36), and she was victorious in 1940 with Roman Hackle and again in 1952 with Mont Tremblant.

FROM THE HORSE'S MOUTH (11)

"Denman is in the box right next to Kauto Star – and it doesn't get closer than that in racing. That's why the build-up to this Gold Cup feels bigger than any I can remember. I'm not going to sleep much between now and next Friday but it's great for the sport."
Paul Nicholls*, speaking before the Cheltenham Gold Cup 2008*

NAMING OF THE DERBY

Had the 12th Earl of Derby (Lord Derby) not won a coin toss with Sir Charles Bunbury the most famous flat race in the world, the Derby, would be known today as the Bunbury. In 1778 the two men, both horse-racing enthusiasts, were sitting looking over Epsom Downs. They decided it was the ideal location for a racecourse, and the first ever flat race was run on Epsom Downs in 1779. The Oaks, named after Lord Derby's estate, was run over 1 mile, 4 furlongs and 10 yards, and was restricted to three-year-old fillies.

Sir Charles and the Earl of Derby also wanted a race that was open to colts and they decided to create one that both colts and fillies could contest, but limited the horses' age to three. However, as both men wanted this race to be named after them, they decided to flip a coin for the naming rights, and it was the Earl of Derby who won the toss.

EVEN THE BEST AREN'T GOOD ENOUGH

The most famous steeplechase in the world, the Grand National, has seen many highly successful jockeys end their careers without ever riding a winner, including Peter Scudamore (third on Corbiere in 1985) and seven-time Champion Jockey John Francome (third on Rough And Tumble in 1979 and runner-up on the same horse in 1980). Tony McCoy, Champion Jockey on 13 occasions, has never finished the Grand National better than third place.

Carl Llewellyn and Ruby Walsh hold the best record of current jockeys, having each won twice. Llewellyn rode Party Politics to victory in 1992 and Earth Summit in 1998, while Walsh was aboard Papillon in 2000 and Hedgehunter in 2005.

RACING JARGON (20)

Evens – when the punter's potential winnings are equal to the stake placed, e.g. a £5 bet at evens will win £5, plus the stake back = £10.

AKA MR ABINGDON

In 1884 Tom Cannon Sr rode Busybody to victory in the 1000 Guineas and Oaks for George Baird. Three years later Baird's Merry Hampton won the Derby, ridden by Jack Watts and trained by Martin Gurry. When he was just eight years old Baird inherited £2 million from his father and a year later inherited another £1 million from an uncle. He then spent the money on making himself the greatest amateur jockey of all time. In 1880 he entered his first races, hunter chases, riding under the name Mr Abingdon, in reference to the name of one of his Scottish estates, so as to prevent his trustees from finding out what he was doing with his £3 million.

Within two years he was riding in both National Hunt and flat races, but in April 1882 he was banned from racing by the National Hunt Committee for threatening to put a fellow rider over the rails. The Jockey Club extended the ban to flat racing, which led him to race in France were the British bans were unenforceable. In 1884 he was reinstated by both British organizing bodies, but by this time he was heavily involved in ownership.

Nicknamed "The Squire", Baird refused to lead Merry Hampton into the winners' enclosure at Epsom, just in case he was snubbed by Jockey Club members. However, despite the thrills owning Classic winners gave him his true passion was riding and in 1889 he rode 61 winners, with 48 of his victories coming against professional jockeys. Baird died at an early age, 31, from malaria contracted in New Orleans, USA, where he had travelled in order to sponsor a prize fight.

RACING SCANDALS (7)

In 1985, the legendary flat racing jockey Lester Piggott was jailed for one year for failing to accurately declare tax on approximately £3.2 million in earnings. The imprisonment of the man popularly known as "The Long Fellow" sent shockwaves throughout the sport.

CLASSICS LINK TO L'ESCARGOT

Gainsborough, winner of the Derby in 1918, Spearmint, winner of the 1906 Derby, St. Frusquin, winner of the 2000 Guineas in 1896 and St. Simon, a three times champion sire in Britain, all form part of the bloodline of 1970 and 1971 Cheltenham Gold Cup winner L'Escargot, who later beat the legendary Red Rum in an epic run-in to win the 1975 Grand National.

VINCENT O'BRIEN

Born on 9 April 1917 in Churchtown, County Cork, Ireland, Dr Michael Vincent O'Brien began training steeplechasers in 1943 at Clashgannife House in Churchtown. His first winner was Oversway, ridden by Noel Sleator, at Limerick on 20 May 1943. O'Brien guided Cottage Rake to complete a hat-trick of Cheltenham Gold Cup wins, 1948–50, and saddled Hatton's Grace to three straight Champion Hurdles, 1949–51. O'Brien notched up 23 winners at the Cheltenham Festival, but his greatest moment over jumps came in 1953 when he trained Early Mist to glory in the Grand National at Aintree, the first of three successive wins in the prestigious race. O'Brien also saddled Alberoni to glory in the 1952 Irish Grand National and the Galway Plate later that same year.

In 1951, O'Brien moved training camps and set up base at Ballydoyle House, Cashel. Over the next three decades the words "Classic winner" and "O'Brien" were synonymous with flat racing. In 1953, Chamier gave him the first of six Irish Derby triumphs. Ballymoss landed the 1957 Irish Derby and English St Leger and, a year later, won the Coronation Cup, Eclipse Stakes, King George VI and Queen Elizabeth Stakes and Prix de l'Arc de Triomphe.

The 1960s brought rich rewards and in 1962 Larkspur gave O'Brien the first of six wins in the Derby. Long Look (1965) and Valoris (1966) claimed back-to-back Oaks wins while Glad Rags (1966) was his only English 1000 Guineas winner. The O'Brien–Lester Piggott partnership landed the first of their four Derby victories with Sir Ivor in 1968. The colt was a magnificent thoroughbred, also winning the English 2000 Guineas and the Washington D.C. International Stakes at Laurel, USA. In 1969–70, Nijinsky continued O'Brien's golden run. During the 1970s O'Brien and Robert Sangster together with Vincent's son-in-law, John Magnier, founded the Coolmore Syndicate, one of the world's most successful horse-racing and breeding operations.

In 1990 O'Brien – voted the greatest figure in the history of horse racing by *Racing Post* readers – coaxed Piggott out of retirement to ride Royal Academy in the Breeders' Cup Mile, with the pair successful once again. O'Brien claimed his last Group 1 winner with Fatherland in the 1992 National Stakes, while fittingly his last ever win came at The Curragh in 1994 with Mysterious Ways.

Did You Know That

Vincent O'Brien married Jacqueline Wittenoom, from Perth, Australia, in 1951. They spend six months in Ireland and six months in Perth.

FIRST DERBY

The inaugural Derby was run in 1780, and the man who lost a coin toss with Lord Derby to have the race named after him, Sir Charles Bunbury, owned the winning horse, Diomed.

SIX RUNNERS BUT NO WINNER

Aidan O'Brien trained six of the 16 runners in the 2008 Oaks. His best-placed finisher was Moonstone, under Richard Hughes, second to Look Here, trained by Ralph Beckett and ridden by Seb Sanders.

		Trainer	*Jockey*
1.	Look Here	R.M. Beckett	Seb Sanders
2.	Moonstone	A.P O'Brien	Richard Hughes
3.	Katiyra (IRE)	John M. Oxx	M.J. Kinane
4.	Clowance	R. Charlton	L. Dettori
5.	Lush Lashes	J.S. Bolger	K.J. Manning
6.	Cape Amber (IRE)	P.W. Chapple-Hyam	Jamie Spencer
7.	Michita (USA)	J.H.M. Gosden	Jimmy Fortune
8.	Savethisdanceforme (IRE)	A.P. O'Brien	C. O'Donoghue
9.	Chinese White (IRE)	D K Weld	P.J. Smullen
10.	Saphira's Fire (IRE)	W.R. Muir	Martin Dwyer
11.	Miracle Seeker	C.G. Cox	Adam Kirby
12.	Sugar Mint (IRE)	B.W. Hills	Michael Hills
13.	Sail (IRE)	A.P. O'Brien	Ryan Moore
14.	Tiffany Diamond (IRE)	A.P. O'Brien	J.A. Heffernan
15.	Adored (IRE)	A.P. O'Brien	J Murtagh
16.	Ice Queen (IRE)	A.P. O'Brien	David McCabe

MICK CALLS IT A DAY

In August 2008 Mick Fitzgerald, who rode Rough Quest to Grand National glory in 1996, announced his retirement as a jockey because of injury. He sustained serious neck and knee injuries after falling from L'Ami in the 2008 National. "I have had to take the advice of the medical experts and they are obviously correct. I've had a great career in racing," said Fitzgerald in an interview with the *Daily Star*. Fitzgerald also landed the 1999 Cheltenham Gold Cup on See More Business. In tribute to Fitzgerald's career, trainer Nicky Henderson, for whom Fitzgerald rode 762 winners, said, "His greatest attribute to us was that he wasn't just a jockey, he was a team player as far as we were concerned and a great mate. His input was enormous."

LADIES OF THE AINTREE COURSE

In 1982 Geraldine Rees on Cheers became the first female jockey to complete the Grand National course. Rosemary Henderson rode her own horse, the 13-year-old Fiddlers Pike, to fifth place in the 1994 race, coming home at 100-1. In 2005 Carrie Ford came home fourth on Forest Gunner priced at 8-1 and, a year later, Nina Carberry finished ninth on the same horse.

RACING JARGON (21)

Bumper – a flat race run over under National Hunt rules – usually over 2 miles – for horses bred for jump racing, but who have not run on the flat. They are designed to give these horses experience of racing against similar animals without having to jump obstacles.

THE RUN FOR THE ROSES

The Kentucky Derby is nicknamed "The Run for the Roses" because the winner is presented with a garland of 554 red roses. The tradition dates back to 1896 and was adopted after New York socialite E. Berry Wall presented roses to ladies at a post-Kentucky Derby party in 1883. The party was attended by Churchill Downs' founder and president, Colonel M. Lewis Clark. The garland and the trophy for winning the race are now presented by the Governor of Kentucky.

Did You Know That?
Dan Fogelberg, an American singer, composed a song entitled "Run for the Roses" for the 1980 running of the race.

OLYMPIC SPORT

By 638 BC thoroughbred horse racing was one of the events in the ancient Greek Olympics.

NORTON'S COIN RIPS UP FORM BOOK

There have been some very long-priced winners of the Cheltenham Gold Cup including the 100-1 winner in 1990 Norton's Coin, the longest odds winner of the race. Incidentally, Norton's Coin is the only Welsh-trained winner of the race. In 1970 L'Escargot won at odds of 33-1, and he won the race again the following year, but this time his odds had shortened considerably, to 7-2.

RULING THE WORLD

Since Godolphin was founded by Sheikh Mohammed bin Rashid Al Maktoum in December 1992. Godolphin horses have run at 119 racecourses worldwide and the stable has produced many Classic winners. The first horse ro run in Godolphin colours was Cutwater, who appeared at Nad Al Sheba on 24 December 1992. Their international operation, at Newmarket, began in 1994. Nad Al Sheba has proved to be Godolphin's most successful course, with 234 winners from 1,003 runners, while Newmarket has been the most successful course in Europe. Here is their top 10 (as of 23 June 2008):

No.	*Racecourse*	*Wins*
1	Nad Al Sheba (UAE)	234
2	Newmarket (UK)	113
3	Goodwood (UK)	63
4	Ascot (UK)	57
5	Doncaster (UK)	52
6	York (UK)	50
7	Belmont Park (USA)	49
8	Longchamp (France)	35
9	Nottingham (UK)	33
10	Lingfield Park (UK)	33

KING OF HENNESSY

Fulke Walwyn is the most successful trainer in the history of the Hennessy Cognac Gold Cup, with seven victories in the race (1957, 1958, 1961, 1963, 1968, 1972 and 1981). Walwyn's final win with Diamond Edge in 1981 came 45 years after he himself rode Reynoldstown to victory in the 1936 Grand National.

Did You Know That?
The last trainer to win back-to-back Hennessy Gold Cups was David Barons in 1986-87.

IRISH 1000 GUINEAS

The Irish 1000 Guineas is a Group 1 flat race that is run in May at The Curragh, County Kildare, Republic of Ireland. The Irish Classic is open to three-year-old fillies and is run over a distance of 1 mile. The inaugural Irish 1000 Guineas was run in 1922 and won by Lady Violette.

FROM THE HORSE'S MOUTH (12)

"I understood that to improve my horses I had to get them properly fit. Horses were fatter and unfit then but I likened them to human athletes – and you never see a fat runner."
***Martin Pipe**, speaking about his early days as a trainer*

DERBY DISTANCE CHANGED

The first four runnings of the Derby were staged over a distance of 1 mile, but in 1884 the race followed the Oaks and was raced over 1 mile, 4 furlongs and 10 yards. This is still the distance that is run today.

FIRST TELEVISED NATIONAL

In 1960 the Grand National was televised live for the very first time by the BBC. Merryman II, ridden by Gerry Scott and trained by Neville Crump, won the race priced as the 13-2 favourite.

THE BOXING HORSE

In 2007 Teofilo, the previous year's champion two-year-old trained in Ireland by Jim Bolger, was priced at only 12-1 by William Hill bookmakers to complete the unique Triple Crown. Bolger named Teofilo after the Cuban triple Olympic heavyweight boxing champion, Teofilo Stevenson, because he felt the horse had similar fighting qualities. But Teofilo, a Galileo colt and winner of all five of his races in 2006 including the Dewhurst Stakes at Newmarket, was withdrawn from the 2000 Guineas just two days before the race after he was found to be sore at the back of a knee. Bookies had Teofilo priced at 2-1 to land the first leg of the Triple Crown and one unhappy Irish punter missed out on an almost certain 50,000 euros payday had Teofilo raced and won the 2000 Guineas having put 2,000 euros on the colt to win the Classic at odds of 25-1 after he won the Futurity Stakes in August 2006.

FLYINGBOLT

In 1966 Flyingbolt, ridden by Pat Taaffe and trained by Tom Dreaper, won the Champion Chase at Cheltenham, at 1-5 the shortest-price winner in the race's history. The next day, he was the 11-8 favourite for the Champion Hurdle and finished third to Salmon Spray.

BAYARDO

Bayardo was one of the outstanding horses of the early 20th century. Foaled in 1906, he won 22 of his 25 races in his career. As a 2-year-old in 1908, he won all seven starts, then 11 out of 13 races aged three, being beaten in the 2000 Guineas (fourth behind Minoru) and the Derby (again beaten by Minoru) but did win the St Leger (ridden by Danny Maher, trained by Alec Taylor Jnr and owned by Alfred W. Cox). Aged four in 1910 he claimed four wins and a second in five races. Bayardo's career earnings were £44,535, while the races he ran in ranged in distance from 5 furlongs to 2½ miles – he was a rare thoroughbred who combined raw speed with enormous stamina.

However, Bayardo will be remembered more for his progeny, which included two Triple Crown-winning sons, Gay Crusader in 1917 and Gainsborough in 1918, and a grandson, Hyperion, winner of the 1933 Derby and St Leger (and champion sire six years in succession), arguably one of the greatest racehorses of all time. He was also the sire of Solario, winner of the 1925 St Leger and 1926 Ascot Gold Cup. At his trainer's Manton Stud he commanded a fee of 300 guineas. Bayardo was the champion sire in 1917 and 1918, and leading broodmare sire in 1925. He died, aged 11, in 1917.

Did You Know That?
Saucy Sue, a granddaughter of Bayardo, won the 1000 Guineas, the Oaks and the Coronation Stakes in 1925.

CHAMPION CHASE FIELDS

The Champion Chase, held as part of the Cheltenham Festival in March, is the most prestigious 2-mile chase on the racing calendar. It was first contested in 1959 and the Queen Mother's name was added to the race title to celebrate the year of her 80th birthday in 1980. The largest field was in 1999, when Call Equiname saw off the challenge of 12 other rivals. The smallest ever field in the race is five runners and occurred in 1961, 1963, 1964, 1968, 1972 and 1985.

TOP 5 BRITISH AND IRISH STUD FEES 2008

1. Galileo....................€225,000
2. Montjeu....................€125,000
3. Danehill Dancer....................€115,000
4. Pivotal....................£85,000
5. Dansili....................£75,000

WINNERS' ENCLOSURE JAM-PACKED

In 2005 Motivator, ridden by Johnny Murtagh and trained by Michael Bell for the Royal Ascot Racing Club syndicate, won the Derby. The lucky syndicate was made up of 230 owners!

RACING JARGON (22)

Walkover – a race with only one horse declared to run.

HORSE OF THE YEAR AWARD

The Horse of the Year Award is an annual award presented to the most outstanding thoroughbred racehorse of the year regardless of age. Since 1991, it has formed part of the Cartier Racing Awards:

Year	*Horse (country of breeding)*
2008	Zarkava (FR)
2007	Dylan Thomas (IRE)
2006	Ouija Board (GB)
2005	Hurricane Run (IRE)
2004	Ouija Board (GB)
2003	Dalakhani (IRE)
2002	Rock of Gibraltar (IRE)
2001	Fantastic Light (USA)
2000	Giant's Causeway (USA)
1999	Daylami (IRE)
1998	Dream Well (FR)
1997	Peintre Celebre (USA)
1996	Helissio (FR)
1995	Ridgewood Pearl (GB)
1994	Barathea (IRE)
1993	Lochsong (GB)
1992	User Friendly (GB)
1991	Arazi (USA)

ANOTHER DOLLY

In 1980, the first year the Champion Chase at Cheltenham had the Queen Mother's name added to it, Another Dolly, ridden by Sam Morshead and trained by Fred Rimell, won at 33-1, the race's longest-priced winner. Another Dolly was only given the race after first past the post Chinrullah had been disqualified for failing a post-race dope test.

GOLD CUP FIVE

Trainer Michael Dickinson trained the first five horses home in the 1983 Cheltenham Gold Cup: Bregawn, Captain John, Wayward Lad, Silver Buck and Ashley House.

IN THE BOOKIES' FAVOUR

In the world of horse racing all bets staked in a race are in essence probability predictions. Therefore, if a horse is at evens the punter has a 50 per cent chance of winning, odds of 1-2 against means the punter has a 33 per cent chance of winning and so on. Taking all the bets placed on the race in total they should ideally add up to 100 per cent, but they can often add up to 130 per cent or higher. Therefore, even if you backed every horse in the race you would still not win any money.

FOOT-AND-MOUTH AT CHELTENHAM

The 2001 Cheltenham Festival was cancelled owing to an outbreak of foot-and-mouth disease.

FROM THE SADDLE TO THE YARD

Since 1900 three Grand National-winning jockeys have also gone on to train the winner of the most famous steeplechase in the world: Algy Anthony (jockey and trainer of Ambush II in 1900 and trainer of Troytown in 1920), Fulke Walwyn (jockey of Reynoldstown in 1936 and trainer of Team Spirit in 1964) and Fred Winter (jockey of Sundew in 1957 and Kilmore in 1962, trainer of Jay Trump in 1965 and Anglo in 1966).

FASTEST EVER KENTUCKY DERBY

The fastest ever Kentucky Derby was the 1973 renewal of the race when Secretariat, ridden by Ron Turcotte, broke the 2-minute mark, coming home in a time of 1 minute 59.4 seconds. Amazingly the runner-up to Secretariat in the race, Sham, 2½ lengths back in second, also dipped under the 2-minute mark, clocking 1 minute 59.8 seconds.

In the 35 Kentucky Derby races run since Secretariat set the record only one other horse has managed to go under 2 minutes – Monarchos, ridden by Jorge F. Chavez clocked 1 minute 59.97 seconds in 2001.

LESTER PIGGOTT

Lester Keith Piggott was born in Wantage on 5 November 1935, the son of Keith Piggott who won the Champion Hurdle in 1939 as a jockey on African Sister and trained the winner of the 1963 Grand National, Ayala. Keith was the British Jump Racing Champion Trainer in 1963. In 1948 a 12-year-old Lester won his first race, on a horse named The Chase at Haydock Park. Over the next 50 years he would go on to dominate the "Sport of Kings" and remains perhaps the greatest jockey of all time. In 1954, aged just 18, he rode the first of his record nine Derby winners, Never Say Die (33-1), an appropriate name as Lester's career would later show.

Looking at the young Piggott many would not have taken him for a jockey as he was quite tall, standing at 5 feet 7½ inches (1.73 metres), hence his nickname "The Long Fellow". Although he could ride at 8 stone 4 pounds when necessary, his normal body weight would have been over 9 stone, and for several years in his early career Lester was successful over hurdles during the winter season. During his career as a jockey the adopted "housewives' choice" rode more than 5,400 winners, which included 465 Group 1 wins (which would have been significantly more if the pattern had been introduced earlier), 30 English Classics and the Prix de l'Arc de Triomphe three times.

In 1970 he achieved immortality when he partnered the legendary Nijinsky to the Triple Crown, the last horse to achieve the coveted title, and won the Champion Jockey title 11 times (1960, 1964–71, 1981 and 1982). Piggott retired from riding horses at the end of the 1985 flat season, and became a racehorse trainer, but in 1987 he was jailed for three years (he served 366 days) for tax evasion. His imprisonment resulted in him being stripped of the OBE he was awarded in 1975. In 1990 Vincent O'Brien famously coaxed him out of retirement and he landed the Breeders' Cup Mile in the USA. In the same year "The Lesters" was inaugurated, an annual awards ceremony for British jockeys, named in honour of The Long Fellow.

Piggott rode his last winner in October 1994, poetically at Haydock Park, before retiring a second time. Despite being admitted to intensive care in a Swiss hospital in May 2007 following a recurrence of a previous heart problem, in June 2008 Lester Piggott attended the Derby and tipped the winner, New Approach, during a BBC television interview.

Did You Know That?

Piggott rode winners in 37 countries outside the United Kingdom.

FROM THE HORSE'S MOUTH (13)

"This is a lovely, lovely day. You can take me round the corner and shoot me now – I don't give a bugger."
***Ginger McCain**, speaking after Amberleigh House's Grand National victory in 2004*

ROCKET POWER

Lammtarra, winner of the 1995 Derby when ridden by Walter Swinburn for trainer Saeed bin Suroor, holds the record for the fastest time recorded in the race – a blistering 2 minutes 32.21 seconds. This time was 1.53 seconds inside the previous best and is a record that still stands today.

IN A CLASS OF HIS OWN

In the past 50 years (1959–2008) only Red Rum has managed to win the Grand National at Aintree and the Scottish Grand National in the same year, doing so in 1974. Merryman II won the Scottish National in 1959 and then won at Aintree the following year; Little Polveir won the Scottish National in 1987 and triumphed round Aintree in 1989, and Earth Summit won the Scottish National in 1994 and the Aintree race in 1998.

RACING JARGON (23)

All-weather racing – racing on the flat on artificial surfaces – either Polytrack or Equitrack – which allows racing to be held all year round.

SUCCESS BREEDS SUCCESS

Nijinsky's success at stud was immediate and quite spectacular, with his stallion fee reaching $300,000 in 1987.

BINDAREE'S MOMENT OF GLORY

When Jim Culloty rode Bindaree to glory in the 2002 Grand National he became the first jockey for 26 years to complete the Cheltenham Gold Cup–Grand National double in the same season. A few weeks earlier Culloty won the Gold Cup aboard Best Mate, but he only got the ride at Aintree a few days before the race when Bindaree's regular jockey, Jamie Goldstein, broke a leg.

IRISH DERBY WINNERS 1946–2008

Year	Winner	Jockey	Trainer
2008	Frozen Fire	S. Heffernan	A.P. O'Brien
2007	Soldier of Fortune	S. Heffernan	A.P. O'Brien
2006	Dylan Thomas	K. Fallon	A.P. O'Brien
2005	Hurricane Run	K. Fallon	A. Fabre
2004	Grey Swallow	P. Smullen	D. Weld
2003	Alamashar	J. Murtagh	J. Oxx
2002	High Chaparral	M. Kinane	A.P. O'Brien
2001	Galileo	M. Kinane	A.P. O'Brien
2000	Sinndar	J. Murtagh	J. Oxx
1999	Montjeu	C. Asmussen	J. Hammond
1998	Dream Well	C. Asmussen	P. Bary
1997	Desert King	C. Roche	A.P. O'Brien
1996	Zagreb	P. Shanahan	D. Weld
1995	Winged Love	O. Peslier	A. Fabre
1994	Balanchine	F. Dettori	H. Ibrahim
1993	Commander in Chief	P. Eddery	H. Cecil
1992	St Jovite	C. Roche	J. Bolger
1991	Generous	A. Munro	P. Cole
1990	Salsabil	W. Carson	J. Dunlop
1989	Old Vic	S. Cauthen	H. Cecil
1988	Kahyasi	R. Cochrane	L. Cumani
1987	Sir Harry Lewis	J. Reid	B.W. Hills
1986	Shahrastani	W.R. Swinburn	M. Stoute
1985	Law Society	P. Eddery	M.V. O'Brien
1984	El Gran Senor	P. Eddery	M.V. O'Brien
1983	Shareef Dancer	W.R. Swinburn	M. Stoute
1982	Assert	C. Roche	D.V. O'Brien
1981	Shergar	L. Piggott	M. Stoute
1980	Tyrnavos	A. Murray	B. Hobbs
1979	Troy	W. Carson	W.R. Hern
1978	Shirley Heights	G. Starkey	J. Dunlop
1977	The Minstrel	L. Piggott	M.V. O'Brien
1976	Malacate	P. Paquet	F. Boutin
1975	Grundy	P. Eddery	P. Walwyn
1974	English Prince	Y. Saint-Martin	P. Walwyn
1973	Weaver's Hall	G. McGrath	S. McGrath
1972	Steel Pulse	W. Williamson	A. Breasley
1971	Irish Ball	A. Gibert	P. Lallié
1970	Nijinsky	L. Ward	M.V. O'Brien
1969	Prince Regent	G. Lewis	E. Pollet

1968	Ribero	L. Piggott	R.F. Johnson Houghton
1967	Ribocco	L. Piggott	R.F. Johnson Houghton
1966	Sodium	F. Durr	G. Todd
1965	Meadow Court	L. Piggott	P.J. Prendergast
1964	Santa Claus	W. Burke	J. M. Rogers
1963	Ragusa	G. Bougoure	P.J. Prendergast
1962	Tambourine	R. Poincelet	E. Pollet
1961	Your Highness	H. Holmes	H.L. Cottrill
1960	Chamour	G. Bougoure	A.S. O'Brien
1959	Fidalgo	J. Mercer	H. Wragg
1958	Sindon	L. Ward	M. Dawson
1957	Ballymoss	T. P. Burns	M. V. O'Brien
1956	Talgo	E. Mercer	H. Wragg
1955	Panaslipper	J. Eddery	S. McGrath
1954	Zarathustra	P. Powell, Jr	M. Hurley
1953	Chamier	W. Rickaby	M.V. O'Brien
1952	Thirteen of Diamonds	J. Mullane	P.J. Prendergast
1951	Fraise du Bois	C. Smirke	H. Wragg
1950	Dark Warrior	J.W. Thompson	P.J. Prendergast
1949	Hindostan	W.R. Johnstone	F. Butters
1948	Nathoo	W.R. Johnstone	F. Butters
1947	Sayajirao	E. Britt	F. Armstrong
1946	Bright News	M. Wing	D. Rogers

HE TRAINED HALF THE FIELD

In 2007 Aidan O'Brien saddled eight of the 17 horses in the Derby. Their finishing positions were:

- Eagle Mountain – 2nd
- Soldier of Fortune – 5th
- Yellowstone – 8th
- Acapulco – 9th
- AdmiraloftheFleet – 10th
- Mahler – 11th
- Anton Chekhov – 12th
- Archipenko – 17th (last)

NO ROSES FOR THESE STARS

Some of the most famous horses in American racing history didn't run in the Kentucky Derby. These include Buckpasser, Cigar, John Henry, Kelso, Man O' War and Seabiscuit.

RED RUM

If asked to think of one name associated with the Grand National, nine out of ten people will say "Red Rum". Rummy, as he was affectionately known, is a national legend who cemented his name among the greatest horses when he won his third Grand National in 1977. The horse, a bay gelding, was foaled on 3 May 1965, sired by Quorum out of Mared. Red Rum's first race was at Aintree, the Thursby Selling Plate in April 1967 when, ridden by Lester Piggott, he dead-heated with Curlicue (Aintree – which had a mixed flat and jumps card for the Grand National meeting – did not have a photo-finish camera at the time) to earn his owner, Maurice Kingsley, the modest sum of £135. Having been owned for five years by Mrs Lurline Brotherton, the horse was put up for sale in August 1972.

Enter Donald "Ginger" McCain. Despite the fact that the horse was suffering from pedalostitis, Ginger purchased Red Rum for Noel Le Mare and it proved to be an inspired outlay of 6,000 guineas. Red Rum's foot problems continued until he ran into the sea on a training gallop at Southport Sands. The salt water appeared to help, so McCain made running in the sea part of Rummy's training regime.

Red Rum's first National was in 1973 and he and Crisp went off as 9-1 joint favourites, but Rummy received 24lbs from the Australian-bred top weight. Crisp led by 30 lengths with two fences to jump, but Brian Fletcher guided Red Rum past the exhausted Crisp in the final few yards to win by a neck in a winning time that shattered the course record by 18 seconds. The following year Red Rum carried top weight (12 stone), but he and Brian Fletcher won again, ahead of the two-times Cheltenham Gold Cup winner L'Escargot.

Despite running well in the 1975 and 1976 Nationals, Red Rum finished second behind L'Escargot and Rag Trade respectively. For the 1977 National, jockey Tommy Stack, who had both ridden and trained Rummy earlier in his career, was booked to ride the 12-year-old horse and steered him to a 25-length victory over Churchtown Boy. Rummy's name was now etched in the history books as the only horse to win the world's most famous steeplechase three times, a feat that may never be equalled. Although entered for the next three Grand Nationals, injuries prevented him from running. However, from 1980, Red Rum went to Aintree and led the parade. He returned every year thereafter until his death on 18 October 1995 aged 30.

Did You Know That?

Red Rum was buried at Aintree, with his head facing the winning post. A statue of Rummy stands near the parade ring at the course.

DERBY'S FIRST FEMALE RIDER

Alex Greaves is the only woman to date to have ridden in the Derby, saddling the filly Portuguese Lil in 1996, which finished in last place (20th). Greaves is Britain's most successful female jockey and rode her first winner, Andrew's First, at Southwell, on 1 December 1989. In 1997 she dead-heated for the Nunthorpe Stakes on Ya Malak to become the first (and to date only) woman to win a Group 1 race in Britain. She won the Lester Award for the best female jockey of the year in 1990, 1991, 1995, 1997 and 1998 and is married to the former jockey and leading trainer David Nicholls.

In March 2000 Greaves failed a drug test after testing positive for a banned diuretic, which aids weight loss. At a Jockey Club hearing in August of the same year the disciplinary committee accepted her explanation that the positive test was as a result of a permissible prescription drug and she was cleared.

RACING JARGON (24)

Colours or silks – the "uniform" worn by a jockey, which are the registered racing colours of the horse's owner.

THE GOLDEN GOLD CUP WINNER

The most successful horse in the history of the Cheltenham Gold Cup is the legendary Golden Miller, who won the race five times in consecutive years from 1932 to 1936. Meanwhile, three other horses have landed the Gold Cup on three occasions in succession: Cottage Rake (1948–50), Arkle (1964–66) and Best Mate (2002–04).

DUTCH LUCK

Dutch jockey Josephine Bruning claimed the first win of her career in a four-horse apprentices' race at Kempton Park on 18 March 2008 when a blunder by three jockeys handed her victory on Sol Rojo. Ross Atkinson, Billy Cray and Paul Nolan allowed Sol Rojo to take the lead in the 1½-mile race, but by the time they realized it was about time to test their mounts, Sol Rojo was already 25 lengths clear with no chance of being caught. However, the 23-year-old Bruning was so unsure that she had actually won the race she decided to carry on riding for the best part of an extra circuit before she was called back in. Sol Rojo won by 16 lengths priced at 14-1. For their tactical blunders Cray and Atkinson were both banned for 12 days and Nolan for 10.

FAVOURITES SHINE

In the past 41 runnings of the Derby (1968–2008) the winner has been the first or second favourite 27 times.

FIRST LADY TO WIN THE NATIONAL

In 1915 Lady Nelson became the first woman to own an Aintree Grand National winner with Ally Sloper, ridden by John Randolph "Jack" Anthony. Not many pundits gave the nine-year-old horse any chance of even completing the Aintree course, let alone winning the race, because he had fallen the previous year. It was Anthony's second victory in the National, having won in 1911 on Glenside. In 1920 he became only the sixth jockey in history to win the race three times after steering Troytown to glory (he also finished runner-up on Old Tay Bridge in 1925 and 1926 and was third on Bright's Boy in 1927). Anthony, a Welshman, rode his first winner in 1906 and was an amateur until 1921, winning the Jockeys' Championship on two occasions, 1914 and 1928. He retired from riding after landing the 1928 title and became a trainer, helping Easter Hero win the Cheltenham Gold Cup in 1929 and 1930. In 1991 Anthony was included in the Welsh Sports Hall of Fame.

ALCOHOL-DRINKING SUPER FILLY

After Pebbles, ridden by Philip Robinson and trained by Clive Brittain, won the 1000 Guineas in 1984 her breeder and owner, Marcos Lemos, sold her to Sheikh Mohammed. Pebbles drank a pint of Guinness each day.

TAKING NO CHANCES

No winner of the Derby has run in the St Leger since Reference Point won both Classics in 1987. One reason is because the owner of a Derby winner can command a high fee for his horse at stud while a loss in the St Leger may damage the horse's value. Another reason is that most modern Derby winners aren't bred to run the 1¾ miles of the St Leger.

DETTORI SENIOR

Wollow won the 2000 Guineas in 1976 to add to his Dewhurst Stakes triumph in 1975, with Gianfranco Dettori, the father of Frankie Dettori, in the saddle both times.

KENTUCKY DERBY TRAGEDY

The 2008 Kentucky Derby was won by Big Brown ahead of the filly Eight Belles. But there was tragedy as the horses slowed down because Eight Belles crumpled to the ground having somehow shattered both ankles. She was immediately euthanized. It was the latest in a series of high-profile Triple Crown tragedies in recent years, following Barbaro's injury in the 2007 Preakness Stakes and Charismatic in the 1999 Belmont Stakes – indeed only Charismatic survived his injuries.

McCOY RULES CHELTENHAM

Tony McCoy's victory in the 2008 Royal & SunAlliance Chase on the 4-1 favourite Alberta's Run was the champion jockey's 20th career win at the Cheltenham Festival. McCoy went on to claim his 13th Jockeys Championship at the end of the 2007–08 season.

MOVE OVER GRANDAD

During the 1960s riding legends Lester Piggott and Scobie Breasley enjoyed a fierce rivalry, with the pair winning the Jockeys' Championship in every year of the decade. The Australian Breasley won three titles in a row, 1961–63, but Piggott claimed it the other seven times, 1960 and 1964–69 inclusive. Both riders were perfectionists and craved to have their mounts by the rails, leading to the odd clash between the pair. Sometimes, during a race Piggott, 21 years younger than the Australian master, would attempt to unsettle his opponent by shouting out, "Move over, Grandad!" The closest Jockeys' Championship race between them came in 1963, and it went down to the final day of the season when Breasley took the coveted crown by a single winner, 176 to 175.

Did You Know That?
Breasley celebrated his wedding to May on 5 November 1935, ironically the same day Piggott was born.

DREAMING WALSH

When six-year-old Ruby Walsh watched his father Ted winning the Foxhunters' Chase at Cheltenham on Attitude Adjuster on television in 1986, he dreamed of winning the Cheltenham Gold Cup. And the dream came true in 2007 when he rode Kauto Star to glory.

SIRE OF DERBY KINGS

Northern Dancer was foaled on 27 May 1961 in Canada. His sire was Nearctic, his dam Natalma, and he was owned by Windfields Farm and bred by Edward P. Taylor. In 1964 the three-year-old dark bay won the Flamingo Stakes, Florida Derby, Blue Grass Stakes, Kentucky Derby (in a record time), Preakness Stakes and Queen's Plate. In the two years he raced Northern Dancer won 14 of his 18 races and never finished worst than third.

After his racing days were over Northern Dancer went on to become the most successful sire of the 20th century, siring 146 stakes winners including three Derby winners: Nijinsky (1970), The Minstrel (1977) and Secreto (1984).

RACING SCANDALS (8)

In October 2002, a BBC TV *Panorama* documentary entitled "The Corruption of Racing" accused horse racing of being "institutionally corrupt" and a "whole generation of jockeys" of having links with organized crime. However, the Jockey Club, which runs horse racing in Britain, dismissed the programme as "a bit of fluff". The claims came from the former head of security at the Jockey Club, Roger Buffham, who intimated that the Jockey Club did not possess the will to pursue offenders, saying, "I presented reports on [one jockey] on at least three occasions. But there was not sufficient resolve or robustness to deal with him." The programme, which took six months to complete, questioned the Jockey Club's effectiveness as the governing body of the sport in Britain and official regulator of the sport. It also included an interview with ex-jockey Dermot Browne, who claimed he doped "about 27 horses" in 1990.

SPONSORED JOCKEYS

In 2004 jockeys riding in the Kentucky Derby were permitted to wear corporate advertising logos on their silks.

ASCOT HISTORY

The racecourse at Ascot was founded by Queen Anne in 1711. The first race, Her Majesty's Plate, was run on 11 August 1711 with a purse of 100 guineas to the winner. Until 1945 the only racing that took place at Ascot was the Royal Meeting. The course is situated on the Ascot Estate, which is owned by Her Majesty Queen Elizabeth II.

FROM THE HORSE'S MOUTH (14)

"You can have your Gold Cups days at Ascot with all those formal up-nosed people, and you can have your Cheltenham with all your country types and the tweeds and whatever – this is a people's place and a people's race."
***Ginger McCain**, after Amerbleigh House's 2004 victory at Aintree*

2000 GUINEAS COPYCATS

The format of the 1000 Guineas has been adopted by many racing authorities around the world, giving birth to such races as the French Jockey Club's Poule d'Essai des Poulains, the Irish 2000 Guineas, Germany's Mehl-Mülhens-Rennen and the Premio Parioli in Italy.

KINANE'S TRIPLE CROWN

When Michael Kinane rode the 13-8 favourite Milan to victory in the 2001 St Leger it was a record seventh European Classic and a 15th Group 1 victory for the Ballydoyle stable in Tipperary. Milan, sired by the legendary Sadler's Wells, was trained by Aidan O'Brien who was following in the footsteps of the godfather of training at the world-famous yard, Vincent O'Brien. "With the wind blowing us around I was happy to stay among horses. I got a bit shut off for a moment but was able to work my way through in my own time. When I really wanted him to he came up with the answers. He was a bit unlucky early in the season, and would have won the French Derby if he hadn't slipped at the start. He goes for the Arc and he would have a chance. He is no mug," said the 42-year-old Kinane, who was riding his eighth English Classic winner on what was his first ever ride in the St Leger.

HOLLYWOOD NATIONAL

In 1963 Ayala won the Grand National but the talk of Aintree that year was the Hollywood heart-throb Gregory Peck, whose horse finished seventh in the race. Different Class, also owned by Peck, finished third in the 1969 National.

RACING JARGON (25)

Placepot – similar to the Jackpot, but the punter's selections only have to be placed, with the same conditions as applied to a place bet.

MARTIN PIPE

Martin Pipe was born on 29 May 1945, the son of a bookmaker. After a brief career as an amateur jockey, he retired to take up training in 1974 at stables in Nicholashayne, near Wellington, Devon. His first winner, called Hit Parade, came in a Taunton selling hurdle in May 1975.

Big-time success was still some way off, but this intensely private man, training away from the glare of publicity, slowly built up his stables. Using an unusually scientific method of getting the best out of his horses – it was considered dubious by many – Pipe first appeared on the radar in 1981 when Baron Blakeney, a 66-1 shot, stormed home in the Cheltenham Trial Hurdle, the first of 32 winners at the Festival. Champion jockeys Peter Scudamore, Richard Dunwoody and Tony McCoy all were stable jockeys for Mr Pipe, who won the Trainers' Championship at the end of every season from 1989 to 1993 and 1996 to 2005 (David Nicholson took the honours in 1994 and 1995).

Pipe saddled 4,183 winners across Europe, most of them in National Hunt races, before before ill health forced his retirement in April 2006. David Pipe took over his father's licence but the winners kept coming.

TONY McCOY'S NATIONAL TALE OF WOE

Tony McCoy may be the most successful jump jockey in history, but he, like many other champion jockeys, has found the Grand National a frustrating race. He rode in every National from 1995 to 2008, except 1997, but only completed the course four times in 13 attempts, never coming closer than third:

Year	*Horse*	*Result*
1995	Chatam	fell at 12th
1996	Deep Bramble	pulled up 29th
1997	*Unable to ride*	
1998	Challenger Du Luc	fell at 1st
1999	Eudipe	fell at 22nd
2000	Dark Stranger	unseated at 3rd
2001	Blowing Wind	finished 3rd
2002	Blowing Wind	finished 3rd
2003	Iris Bleu	pulled up 16th
2004	Jurancon II	fell at 4th
2005	Clan Royal	carried out 22nd
2006	Clan Royal	finished 3rd
2007	L'Ami	finished 10th
2008	Butler's Cabin	fell at 22nd

MASTERS OF AINTREE

Two trainers share the record for most Grand National wins with four:

Fred Rimell	Donald "Ginger " McCain
E.S.B. (1956)	Red Rum (1973, 1974, 1977)
Nicolaus Silver (1961)	Amberleigh House (2004)
Gay Trip (1970)	
Rag Trade (1976)	

OVER THREE CONTINENTS

Angel A. Penna Sr was born in Argentina and trained racehorses in South America, North America and Europe. His career as a trainer began in 1950 and over the next 40 years he had more than 250 graded stakes winners. From his stables in France he trained horses for the wealthy French art dealer, Daniel Wildenstein. In 1972 Penna won the Prix de l'Arc de Triomphe with the filly San San and repeated the success in 1974 with the legendary filly Allez France. Penna also won three English Classics for Wildenstein, the Oaks with Pawnese in 1976 (who also won the 1976 King George VI and Queen Elizabeth Stakes), the 1000 Guineas in 1976 with Flying Water and the 1976 St Leger with Crow (who also won the Coronation Cup in 1978).

Did You Know That?
Allez France was the first filly in thoroughbred horse-racing history to earn $1 million ($1,386,146), winning 13 of her 21 races.

RACING JARGON (26)

Flat racing – the turf flat season usually begins in late March, with the Lincoln meeting at Doncaster, and ends in early November. The all-weather season runs from November to March.

ARC DOUBLE FOR ALLEGED

In 1977 Dunfermline, ridden by Willie Carson, trained by Dick Hern and owned by Queen Elizabeth II, won the St Leger and thus inflicted the only defeat suffered by Alleged. Alleged, ridden by Lester Piggott and trained by Vincent O'Brien, finished second, but went on to win the Prix de l'Arc de Triomphe in consecutive years (1977 and 1978), the last horse to achieve the feat. His Timeform rating of 138 puts him among the greatest racehorses of all time.

CHELTENHAM GOLD CUP 1946–2008

The Cheltenham Gold Cup is a Grade 1 steeplechase run at Cheltenham for horses aged five and over and is run over a distance of 3 miles 2½ furlongs with 22 fences to be negotiated. The race is run during the Cheltenham Festival in March.

Year	*Winner*	*Jockey*	*Trainer*
2008	Denman	Sam Thomas	Paul Nicholls
2007	Kauto Star	Ruby Walsh	Paul Nicholls
2006	War of Attrition	Conor O'Dwyer	Mouse Morris
2005	Kicking King	Barry Geraghty	Tom Taaffe
2004	Best Mate	Jim Culloty	Henrietta Knight
2003	Best Mate	Jim Culloty	Henrietta Knight
2002	Best Mate	Jim Culloty	Henrietta Knight
2001**	*no race*		
2000	Looks Like Trouble	Richard Johnson	Noel Chance
1999	See More Business	Mick Fitzgerald	Paul Nicholls
1998	Cool Dawn	Andrew Thornton	Robert Alner
1997	Mr Mulligan	Tony McCoy	Noel Chance
1996	Imperial Call	Conor O'Dwyer	Fergie Sutherland
1995	Master Oats	Norman Williamson	Kim Bailey
1994	The Fellow	Adam Kondrat	François Doumen
1993	Jodami	Mark Dwyer	Peter Beaumont
1992	Cool Ground	Adrian Maguire	Toby Balding
1991	Garrison Savannah	Mark Pitman	Jenny Pitman
1990	Norton's Coin	Graham McCourt	Sirrel Griffiths
1989	Desert Orchid	Simon Sherwood	David Elsworth
1988	Charter Party	Richard Dunwoody	David Nicholson
1987	The Thinker	Ridley Lamb	Arthur Stephenson
1986	Dawn Run	Jonjo O'Neill	Paddy Mullins
1985	Forgive 'N' Forget	Mark Dwyer	Jimmy FitzGerald
1984	Burrough Hill Lad	Phil Tuck	Jenny Pitman
1983	Bregawn	Graham Bradley	Michael Dickinson
1982	Silver Buck	Robert Earnshaw	Michael Dickinson
1981	Little Owl	Mr Jim Wilson	Peter Easterby
1980*	Master Smudge	Richard Hoare	Arthur Barrow
1979	Alverton	Jonjo O'Neill	Peter Easterby
1978	Midnight Court	John Francome	Fred Winter
1977	Davy Lad	Dessie Hughes	Mick O'Toole
1976	Royal Frolic	John Burke	Fred Rimell
1975	Ten Up	Tommy Carberry	Jim Dreaper
1974	Captain Christy	Bobby Beasley	Pat Taaffe

♀

1973	The Dikler	Ron Barry	Fulke Walwyn
1972	Glencaraig Lady	Frank Berry	Francis Flood
1971	L'Escargot	Tommy Carberry	Dan Moore
1970	L'Escargot	Tommy Carberry	Dan Moore
1969	What a Myth	Paul Kelleway	Ryan Price
1968	Fort Leney	Pat Taaffe	Tom Dreaper
1967	Woodland Venture	Terry Biddlecombe	Fred Rimell
1966	Arkle	Pat Taaffe	Tom Dreaper
1965	Arkle	Pat Taaffe	Tom Dreaper
1964	Arkle	Pat Taaffe	Tom Dreaper
1963	Mill House	Willie Robinson	Fulke Walwyn
1962	Mandarin	Fred Winter	Fulke Walwyn
1961	Saffron Tartan	Fred Winter	Don Butchers
1960	Pas Seul	Bill Rees	Bob Turnell
1959	Roddy Owen	Bobby Beasley	Danny Morgan
1958	Kerstin	Stan Hayhurst	Verly Bewicke
1957	Linwell	Michael Scudamore	Charlie Mallon
1956	Limber Hill	Jimmy Power	Bill Dutton
1955	Gay Donald	Tony Grantham	Jim Ford
1954	Four Ten	Tommy Cusack	John Roberts
1953	Knock Hard	Tim Molony	Vincent O'Brien
1952	Mont Tremblant	Dave Dick	Fulke Walwyn
1951	Silver Fame	Martin Molony	George Beeby
1950	Cottage Rake	Aubrey Brabazon	Vincent O'Brien
1949	Cottage Rake	Aubrey Brabazon	Vincent O'Brien
1948	Cottage Rake	Aubrey Brabazon	Vincent O'Brien
1947	Fortina	Mr Richard Black	Hector Christie
1946	Prince Regent	Tim Hyde	Tom Dreaper

* *Tied Cottage finished first in the 1980 race but was subsequently disqualified after testing positive for a banned substance.*

** *The race was cancelled due to the foot-and-mouth epidemic.*

A FINE TIME WAS HAD BY ALL

At the 2008 Royal Ascot meeting racegoers drank 170,000 bottles of champagne, washed their drinks down with 172 tonnes of ice and ate 4 tonnes of beef, 10,000 lobsters and 100,000 scones.

THE BOYS' RACE

Only three fillies have managed to win the Kentucky Derby: Regret in 1915, Genuine Risk in 1980 and Winning Colors in 1988.

MOST NATIONAL FINISHERS

The highest number of horses ever to finish the Grand National is 23 and this happened in 1984. Hallo Dandy, ridden by Neale Doughty and trained by Gordon W. Richards, won the race ahead of Greasepaint who finished runner-up for the second year running. Richards also trained the 1978 National winner Lucius.

RACING JARGON (27)

Distances – literally the gap between horses at the winning post. Although it is still recorded in lengths, time is measured to define the distances, 0.2 seconds per length in flat races and 0.25 seconds per length in jumps..If a horse wins by 30 or more lengths then it is said to have won the race by a "distance". Meanwhile, distances shorter than a quarter of a length can be a neck, a head, a short head and a nose.

ON THE HOUSE

John Reid, from Banbridge, Northern Ireland, landed his first English Classic in 1982, the 1000 Guineas riding On the House. Other big wins came on Dr. Devious in the 1992 Derby, aboard Tony Bin in the 1988 Prix de l'Arc de Triomphe, the King George VI and Queen Elizabeth Stakes twice, on Ile de Bourbon in 1978 and Swain in 1997 and with Nedawi the 1998 St Leger. Reid was awarded an MBE for his services to the sport in 1997 and when he retired in September 2001 he was appointed president of the Jockeys Association. In total, Reid rode 1,937 winners in the UK and 48 in international Group 1 races.

WORLD RACEHORSE RANKINGS

In 2003 the International Federation of Horseracing Authorities (IFHA) was formed. It is responsible for producing the World Thoroughbred Racehorse Rankings (WTRR). The IFHA is located in France, and is made up of members from all over the world. In 2004 the IFHA compiled its first ever list of the world's best racehorses:

Year	*Horse*	*Country bred*	*Country trained*	*IFHA rating*
2008	Curlin	USA	USA	130
2007	Manduro	Germany	France	131
2006	Invasor	Argentina	USA	129
2005	Hurricane Run	Ireland	France	130
2004	Ghostzapper	USA	USA	130

TIC-TAC

Tic-tac is the complex sign language used by bookmakers at racecourses to converse with one another concerning movements in the price of a horse. Tic-tac men are usually seen standing on a crate or a chair wearing white gloves, frantically waving their hands in the air. The "secret" language is further encoded by the use of what is known as the "Twist Card", which effectively jumbles the racecard numbers for use by specific bookies. Tic-tac prices have their own slang terms, for example:

Straight-up – Evens
Ear'ole – 6-4
Shoulder – 7-4
Top of the head – 9-4
Face – 5-2
Carpet – 3-1
Burlington Bertie/Scruffy and Dirty – 100-30
Rouf (which is four spelled backwards) – 4-1
Shoulders – 9-2
Hand (or Ching) – 5-1
Net (which is ten spelled backwards) – 10-1
Double carpet – 33-1
No hoper – 50-1

Did You Know That?
Channel 4's racing expert, Jim McGrath, is also managing director of Timeform, having joined the company after leaving school in 1974. His first job with the company was putting the glue on cards.

FROM THE HORSE'S MOUTH (15)

"Once you put on their racing plates, the horses know they are going to be in a race, and they look forward to the thrill, some more than others."
Jenny Pitman*, expressing her view as to whether horses know they're in a race*

LUCKY NUMBER 28

When Sir Gordon Richards finally won the Derby in 1953 aboard Pinza it was the legendary jockey's 28th and final attempt to claim the coveted prize.

SEABISCUIT

Seabiscuit was foaled at the Wheatley Stable at Claiborne Farm, Paris, Kentucky, on 23 May 1933, by Hard Tack out of Swing On. His paternal grandsire was Man O'War and his maternal grandsire, Whisk Broom II. Despite his impressive bloodlines the Wheatley family did not rate Seabiscuit highly. He was owned by Gladys Mills Phipps and trained by James "Sunny Jim" Fitzsimmons. Although Fitzsimmons recognized some talent in the knobbly-kneed colt, he afforded most of his time to training Omaha, the 1935 US Triple Crown winner. Indeed, Fitzsimmons felt that Seabiscuit was quite lazy and used him mainly as a workmate to Omaha.

It was not until his 18th career start that he won a race, winning at Narragansett, Rhode Island, on 22 June 1935. As a two-year-old, Seabiscuit raced 35 times, winning five and finishing second seven times. When he turned three, the horse was sold to motor vehicle entrepreneur Charles S. Howard for $8,000. Fitzsimmons knew that the horse had not lived up to his bloodline potential.

At Howard's stable Seabiscuit was trained by Tom Smith and paired with jockey Red Pollard. On 22 August 1936, he ran for the first time under Smith's guidance with Pollard at the controls, but failed to win. However, in his next eight starts he won several times. In November he won the Bay Bridge Handicap run over 1 mile. Despite carrying the top weight (116 pounds) he won by 5 lengths in a time only 3/5-second off the world record. In his next race he won the World's Fair Handicap. In 1937 his seven consecutive Stakes victories tied the record while his 11 wins from 15 starts made him the leading money winner in the USA. His victories earned him celebrity status and he became the "People's Champion".

However, in the same year War Admiral won the US Triple Crown and the coveted Eclipse Award for Horse of the Year. On 1 November 1938, the "Match of the Century" took place at Pimlico Racecourse when Seabiscuit finally met War Admiral. An estimated 40,000 fans were at the track. War Admiral was the overwhelming 1-4 favourite but it was Seabiscuit who won the race.

Seabiscuit ended his career with 33 wins from 89 starts, 15 second places and 13 third places, with career earnings of $437,730. His story has been the subject of two Hollywood movies, the first in 1949 and the second in 2003.

Did You Know That?

In 1938 more newspaper column inches were devoted to Seabiscuit than any other figure – Roosevelt was second and Hitler third.

HIGH-RISE ODDS WINNER

High-Rise, ridden by Olivier Peslier, trained by Luca Cumani and owned by Obaid Al Maktoum, won the 1998 Derby priced at 20-1. He is the last double figure-priced winner of the Classic.

ADD A "W"

Gordon Richards' middle initial, W, was allegedly inserted in his name by an official at Salisbury at the start of his career as a jockey to differentiate him from the legendary Sir Gordon Richards.

THE PRINCE OF PRINCES

Prince Palatine, bred by William Hall Walker, won the 1911 St Leger ridden by Frank O'Neill, trained by Henry Beardsley and owned by Thomas Pilkington. Aged two he won three of his six starts and at three years old he won the St Leger by a comfortable 6 lengths. Prince Palatine was the dominant horse in British racing in 1912 and 1913. Towards the end of the 1913 racing season Thomas Pilkington sold him for a then world record price of £45,000 to Jack B. Joel to stand at his Childwickbury Stud situated in St Albans, Hertfordshire. At the time he had also won the Imperial Produce Plate (1910), Eclipse Stakes (1912), Jockey Club Stakes (1912), Ascot Gold Cup (1912 and 1913), Doncaster Cup (1913), Coronation Cup (1913) and was the British Horse of the Year in 1912 and 1913.

His progeny included Rose Prince, who produced the Belgian Champion Prince Rose, whose descendants included Canonero II (winner of the Kentucky Derby and Preakness Stakes in 1971) and British Horse of the Year winners Mill Reef and Brigadier Gerard. Sadly Prince Palatine died in a stable fire in the USA in 1924.

O'BRIEN CLOSE TO ICONIC STATUS

On 9 June 2001, Aidan O'Brien, aged 31, took another big step on the path to legendary status in Ireland after completing the Oaks–Derby double. The previous day the filly Imagine won the Oaks for O'Brien with Michael Kinane at the controls. Kinane then rode the superb Galileo to glory in the Derby for O'Brien's Ballydoyle Stables, O'Brien's first victory in the world's most famous Classic race. It was Kinane's second triumph in the race, having won on Commander in Chief in 1993.

SIR GORDON RICHARDS

Gordon Richards was born on 5 May 1904 in Donnington Wood, Shropshire. His father raised pit ponies at the family home and Gordon fell in love with horses at an early age. He started riding the ponies bareback when he was seven years old and drove the pony and trap passenger service operated by his father between Wrockwardine Wood and Oakengates Railway Station. Many racing commentators attributed his unique riding style – his use of a long rein and an upright position in the saddle – to his days riding the pony and trap.

Richards left school aged 15. He became a stable boy at Fox Hollies Stable and began his apprenticeship to Martin Hartigan. In March 1921 Richards claimed his first winner, riding Gay Lord to glory at Leicester. After turning professional he won the Champion Jockey title in his rookie season of 1925, riding 118 winners while being retained by Thomas Hogg. However, the following year he contracted tuberculosis and had to sit most of the season out.

Richards returned to riding in December 1926 and reclaimed the championship in 1927. In 1930 Hogg and Richards teamed up for Richards' first Classic success, on Rose of England in the Oaks. However, 1930 was the only uninterrupted campaign in which Richards was not Champion Jockey, Freddie Fox snatching it by one win. In 1932 he became stable jockey to Fred Darling and in 1933 rode 259 winners, a new record, passing the 246 set by the legendary Fred Archer in 1885. In 1942 he won four of the five English Classics, but the one race he wanted to win most of all, the Derby, still eluded him. At the end of the Second World War Richards joined Noel Murless's stable. In 1947 he broke his own record for the most wins in a season when he won 269 races.

By the time 1953 came around Richards decided to retire at the end of the season. Since his first professional season in 1925 he had lost the Champion Jockey title only three times up to the start of his last season in the saddle. So, this would be his 28th and final attempt to land the Derby, partnered with Pinza. In the lead-up to the race Richards became the first, and to date only, jockey to receive a knighthood. His career had a fairytale ending – he won the Derby and the jockeys' title.

In total, Richards had 4,870 winners from 21,843 professional rides. He died on 10 November 1988.

Did You Know That?
The Champion Jockey pub in Donnington, Shropshire, is named in his honour.

BEST HORSE NEVER TO WIN THE DERBY

Shahrastani, ridden by Walter Swinburn, beat Dancing Brave, ridden by Greville Starkey, by half a length to win the 1986 Derby at Epsom. Sitting at the back of the field Dancing Brave – a 2-1 favourite to make it a 2000 Guineas–Derby double – passed 14 horses but failed to catch Shahrastani. However, later in the season, Dancing Brave exacted revenge on Shahrastani by winning both the King George VI and Queen Elizabeth Diamond Stakes at Ascot and the Prix de l'Arc de Triomphe at Longchamps (ridden by Pat Eddery in both races), while Shahrastani could only manage fourth place in both races.

Dancing Brave's victory at Longchamps earned him the title of Europe's Horse of the Year for 1986 and a highest ever rating of 141 since the International Classifications (the official annual league table of top-class flat horses) began in 1977. He raced for the last time in the 1986 Breeders' Cup in Santa Anita but dehydrated badly before the race under the California sun and finished fourth. Dancing Brave, whose grandsire was Northern Dancer, is considered by many to be the best horse never to have won the Derby.

WHIZZING ROUND AINTREE

The fastest time ever recorded by a Grand National winner was by Mr Frisk in 1990. with a blistering mark of 8m 47.8s over the 30 obstacles around Aintree. Mr Frisk was ridden by the amateur jockey Marcus Armytage and carried 10st 6lb on firm ground. Mr Frisk's winning time beat the previous record set by Red Rum in 1973, when he clocked 9m 1.9s in beating Crisp. Rummy, with Brian Fletcher in the saddle, carried 10st 5lb that day.

RACING JARGON (28)

Favourite – the horse in the race with the shortest odds (sometimes referred to as the "jolly").

IRISH 2000 GUINEAS

The Irish 2000 Guineas is a Group 1 flat race that is run in May at The Curragh, County Kildare, Republic of Ireland. The Irish Classic is open to three-year-old thoroughbred colts and fillies and is run over a distance of 1 mile. The inaugural Irish 2000 Guineas was run in 1921 and was won by Soldennis.

KENTUCKY DERBY WINNERS 1946–2008

Year	*Winner*	*Jockey*	*Trainer*
2008	Big Brown	K. Desormeaux	R. Dutrow
2007	Street Sense	C. Borel	C. Nafzger
2006	Barbaro	E. Prado	M.R. Matz
2005	Giacomo	M. Smith	J. Shirreffs
2004	Smarty Jones	S. Elliott	J. Servis
2003	Funny Cide	J. Santos	B. Tagg
2002	War Emblem	V. Espinoza	B. Baffert
2001	Monarchos	J. Chavez	J.T. Ward Jr
2000	Fusaichi Pegasus	K. Desormeaux	N. Drysdale
1999	Charismatic	C. Antley	D.W. Lukas
1998	Real Quiet	K. Desormeaux	B. Baffert
1997	Silver Charm	G. Stevens	B. Baffert
1996	Grindstone	J. Bailey	D.W. Lukas
1995	Thunder Gulch	G. Stevens	D.W. Lukas
1994	Go For Gin	C. McCarron	N. Zito
1993	Sea Hero	J. Bailey	M. Miller
1992	Lil E. Tee	P. Day	L. Whiting
1991	Strike The Gold	C. Antley	N. Zito
1990	Unbridled	C. Perret	C. Nafzger
1989	Sunday Silence	P. Valenzuela	C. Whittingham
1988	Winning Colors	G. Stevens	D.W. Lukas
1987	Alysheba	C. McCarron	J.C. Van Berg
1986	Ferdinand	W. Shoemaker	C. Whittingham
1985	Spend A Buck	A. Cordero Jr	C. Gambolati
1984	Swale	L. Pincay Jr	W.C. Stephens
1983	Sunny's Halo	E. Delahoussaye	D. C. Cross
1982	Gato Del Sol	E. Delahoussaye	E. Gregson
1981	Pleasant Colony	J. Velasquez	J.P. Campo
1980	Genuine Risk	J. Vasquez	L. Jolley
1979	Spectacular Bid	R. Franklin	G.G. Delp
1978	Affirmed	S. Cauthen	L.S. Barrera
1977	Seattle Slew	J. Cruguet	W.H. Turner
1976	Bold Forbes	A. Cordero Jr	L.S. Barrera
1975	Foolish Pleasure	J. Vasquez	L. Jolley
1974	Cannonade	A. Cordero Jr	W.C. Stephens
1973	Secretariat	R. Turcotte	L. Laurin
1972	Riva Ridge	R. Turcotte	L. Laurin
1971	Canonero II	G. Avila	J. Arias
1970	Dust Commander	M. Manganello	D. Combs
1969	Majestic Prince	B. Hartack	J. Longden

1968	Forward Pass	I. Valenzuela	H. Forrest
1967	Proud Clarion	B. Ussery	L. Gentry
1966	Kauai King	D. Brumfield	H. Forrest
1965	Lucky Debonair	W. Shoemaker	L. Gentry
1964	Northern Dancer	B. Hartack	H. Forrest
1963	Chateaugay	B. Baeza	F. Catrone
1962	Decidedly	B. Hartack	H. A. Luro
1961	Carry Back	J. Sellers	J. A. Price
1960	Venetian Way	B. Hartack	V.J. Sovinski
1959	Tomy Lee	W. Shoemaker	F. Childs
1958	Tim Tam	I. Valenzuela	H.A. Jones
1957	Iron Liege	B. Hartack	H.A. Jones
1956	Needles	D. Erb	H.L. Fontaine
1955	Swaps	W. Shoemaker	M.A. Tenney
1954	Determine	R. York	W. Molter
1953	Dark Star	H. Moreno	E. Hayward
1952	Hill Gail	E. Arcaro	B.A. Jones
1951	Count Turf	C. McCreary	S. Rutchick
1950	Middleground	W. Boland	M. Hirsch
1949	Ponder	S. Brooks	B.A. Jones
1948	Citation	E. Arcaro	B.A. Jones
1947	Jet Pilot	E. Guerin	T. Smith
1946	Assault	W. Mehrtens	M. Hirsch

THERE FOR ALL TO SEE

In 1895 the Derby became the first horse race to be filmed. The first radio coverage of the Derby took place in 1927 and in 1932 the Epsom Classic was the first horse race to be televised.

FRISKEY FRISK

At the same time as Mr Frisk was whizzing to victory in the 1990 Grand National a horse named Mr Friskey won his 16th consecutive race in the USA to equal the record set by Citation.

SHARING THE PURSE

Up until the 2004 Kentucky Derby only the first four horses across the finish line received a share of the race purse. However, in 2005 the rules were changed so that the fifth-placed horse also received a share of the spoils.

FROM THE HORSE'S MOUTH (16)

"The Classic for us Europeans is the biggest, most prestigious race you can ever win. I came close twice and I still have to pinch myself I've done it now."
Frankie Dettori*, on his success on Raven's Pass in the 2008 Breeders' Cup Classic*

BREAKING OUT OF THE STALLS

In 1967 starting stalls were used for the Derby for the first time, when the race was won by Royal Palace, trained by Noel Murless and ridden by George Moore.

SMALL STAR OF THE TURF

In 1959 Petite Etoile (meaning "Small Star"), owned by Prince Aly Khan and trained by Noel Murless, won the 1000 Guineas, the Oaks and the Champion Stakes (the first of Lester Piggott's post-war record of five Champion Stakes successes). The following year she comfortably defeated the 1959 Derby winner, Parthia, but lost the King George VI and Queen Elizabeth Diamond Stakes to Aggressor. As a five-year-old she landed a second Coronation Cup and won three other races. When she retired she had won 14 races with total prize money of £72,626. However, despite her success on the track she was a failure as a broodmare.

RACING JARGON (29)

Starting price (SP) – these are the odds at which almost all bets not on the Tote are settled and usually represent the general price being offered in the betting ring on the racecourse before the off.

IRISH OAKS

The Irish Oaks is a Group 1 flat race that is run in July at The Curragh, County Kildare. The Irish Classic is open to three-year-old fillies and is run over a distance of 1 mile, 4 furlongs. The inaugural Irish Oaks was run in 1895 over a distance of 1 mile and was won by Sapling. The race was converted to its present distance of 1 mile, 4 furlongs in 1915, and was won by Latharna. Since 2000, Ouija Board (2004) and Alexandrova (2006) have won the Oaks at both Epsom and The Curragh.

RED RUM ON THE SILVER SCREEN

In the 1980 movie *The Shining*, starring Jack Nicholson, the character Danny uttered the words "Redrum" several times. The 1987 movie *Good Morning Vietnam* starred Robin Williams and was based on Pentagon lawyer Adrian Cronauer's life as a DJ during the Vietnam War. During one of his manic on-air riffs Cronauer continually repeats "Redrum". Episode number 167 (season 8) of the popular US television show *The X-Files* is entitled "Redrum". "Redrum" is the 13th episode in the seventh season of the popular American television crime drama *CSI: Crime Scene Investigation*. In the US TV show *Buffy the Vampire Slayer*, "Redrum" was used by the character Xander as a joke in episode nine of season one, "The Puppet Show". And the word "Redrum" was spelt out in blocks by the character Stewie in an episode of *Family Guy* ("Love Thy Trophy") and by Maggie in an episode of *The Simpsons* ("Treehouse of Horror V").

Did You Know That?
Redrum, a melodic rock band, was formed in 2002. "Red Rum" is also the name of a song on the heavy metal band Lizzy Borden's album *Love You To Pieces*.

RACING SCANDALS (9)

On 29 November 2002, jockey Graham Bradley was banned from racing for eight years by the Jockey Club for bringing the name of the sport into disrepute. Bradley was handed the ban after he admitted that he had received money for passing on "privileged and sensitive racing information" to the infamous "Mr Fixit" – the cocaine smuggler Brian Wright. In 1982 Bradley was suspended for two months by the Jockey Club for placing a bet whilst in the ring. In 1987 he was banned from racing for three months for not trying on Deadly Going in a race at Market Rasen and in 1999 he was arrested and charged as part of a long-running investigation into alleged race fixing although these charges were later dropped. Bradley won the Hennessy Cognac Gold Cup in 1982 and the Cheltenham Gold Cup in 1983. Bradley's autobiography *The Wayward Lad* was published in 2000.

WILLIE'S COSTLY ERROR

In the 1957 Kentucky Derby the American jockey Willie Shoemaker mistakenly pulled up his mount Gallant Man 110 yards before the finish line and was passed by Iron Liege.

DETTORI DAY AT THE DERBY

Frankie Dettori, arguably one of the greatest ever jockeys, finally ended his Derby jinx in 2007 at his 15th attempt by riding the 5-4 favourite Authorized to a 5-length victory over second-placed Eagle Mountain (6-1), with the Aqaleem (9-1) back in third place. The spotlight had been on Dettori throughout the week leading up to the race, with the question being whether or not he could finally get the monkey off his back and win a Derby. Authorized had become favourite for the race after a very impressive win in the Dante Stakes at York. At Epsom, Dettori guided the Peter Chapple-Hyam-trained horse to the front 2 furlongs out and drove him well clear of his 16 challengers. It completed Dettori's sweep of winning all of British horse racing's Classic races.

Dettori celebrated in style on the winners' podium as he jumped on top of the trophy table and waved his trophy in the air much to the delight of his vociferous fans. He then beckoned his father, himself a former jockey, on to the podium to celebrate his first Derby success.

RACING JARGON (30)

Racing certainty – a horse that the bookmakers and the punters alike believe cannot lose a race.

LAST US TRIPLE CROWN SUCCESS

Double Epsom Derby-winning jockey Steve Cauthen (Slip Anchor in 1985 and Reference Point in 1987) rode Affirmed to US Triple Crown glory in 1978 (the Kentucky Derby, the Preakness Stakes and the Belmont Stakes). Affirmed, the 11th and – to date – last horse to achieve the feat, was the great-great-grandson of the legendary 1937 US Triple Crown winner, War Admiral.

BACK-TO-BACK GOLD CUPS

Only six horses in history have won back-to-back Gold Cups at Cheltenham. The most recent was Best Mate who claimed three in a row from 2002 to 2004. Prior to Best Mate's domination of the race no other horse had won back-to-back Gold Cups since L'Escargot did it in 1970 and 1971. The other four horses to have done so are Easter Hero (1929 and 1930), Golden Miller (1932–36), Cottage Rake (1948–50) and Arkle (1964–66).

GIRL WINS THE GRAND NATIONAL

A fictional account of a young girl riding the winner of the Aintree Grand National written by Enid Bagnold was made into a movie in 1944 entitled *National Velvet*. The movie starred a young Elizabeth Taylor as the heroine, Velvet Brown, with Mickey Rooney playing the trainer of her horse, The Pie.

HISTORY REWRITTEN

In 2001 the victory of the champion stallion Sadler's Wells filly, Imagine (ridden by Michael Kinane, trained by Aidan O'Brien and owned by Diane Nagle & Sue Magnier), in the Oaks set a new record for top-class winners sired by one horse. Imagine's victory at Epsom meant that Sadler's Wells had produced the winners of 47 individual Group 1 races and put the American-bred stallion one ahead of the New Zealand sire Sir Tristram, who died in 1997. Added to that, Sadler's Wells achieved the rare distinction of having produced the first three home in the fillies' Classic, with Queen Elizabeth II's horse Flight of Fancy second and Relish The Thought coming home in third place. Imagine was also his fourth Oaks winner following Salsabil (1990), Intrepidity (1993) and Moonshell (1995).

Did You Know That?
The day after Imagine's success, Galileo provided Sadler's Wells with his first Derby winner.

CHAMPION HURDLE–GOLD CUP DOUBLE

Only one horse has managed to win the most prestigious hurdle and steeplechase races on the British National Hunt calendar. The Irish mare Dawn Run won the Champion Hurdle in 1984 and the Gold Cup in 1986. Dawn Run was trained by Paddy Mullins and ridden by Jonjo O'Neill in both races.

A different sort of "double" was achieved in 1995. Alderbrook won the Champion Hurdle and Master Oats was victorious in the Gold Cup. Both horses were trained by Kim Bailey and ridden by Norman Williamson, but this was the fifth trainer–jockey double.

PAIN IN THE FOOT

For most of his life Red Rum suffered from a debilitating, incurable bone disease in his foot.

CHAMPION FLAT JOCKEYS 1945–2008

(No. of winners in parentheses)

2008	R. Moore (186)
2007	S. Sanders (190)
	J. Spencer (190)
2006	R. Moore (180)
2005	J. Spencer (163)
2004	L. Dettori (192)
2003	K. Fallon (207)
2002	K. Fallon (136)
2001	K. Fallon (166)
2000	K. Darley (155)
1999	K. Fallon (200)
1998	K. Fallon (204)
1997	K. Fallon (202)
1996	P. Eddery (186)
1995	L. Dettori (216)
1994	L. Dettori (233)
1993	P. Eddery (169)
1992	M. Roberts (206)
1991	P. Eddery (165)
1990	P. Eddery (209)
1989	P. Eddery (171)
1988	P Eddery (183)
1987	S. Cauthen (197)
1986	P. Eddery (176)
1985	S. Cauthen (195)
1984	S. Cauthen (130)
1983	W. Carson (159)
1982	L. Piggott (188)
1981	L. Piggott (179)
1980	W. Carson (165)
1979	J. Mercer (164)
1978	W. Carson (182)
1977	P .Eddery (176)
1976	P. Eddery (162)
1975	P. Eddery (164)
1974	P. Eddery (148)
1973	W. Carson (163)
1972	W. Carson (132)
1971	L. Piggott (162)
1970	L. Piggott (162)
1969	L. Piggott (163)
1968	L. Piggott (139)
1967	L. Piggott (117)
1966	L. Piggott (191)
1965	L. Piggott (166)
1964	L. Piggott (140)
1963	A. Breasley (176)
1962	A. Breasley (179)
1961	A. Breasley (171)
1960	L. Piggott (170)
1959	D. Smith (157)
1958	D. Smith (165)
1957	A. Breasley (173)
1956	D. Smith (155)
1955	D. Smith (168)
1954	D. Smith (129)
1953	G. Richards (191)
1952	G. Richards (231)
1951	G. Richards (227)
1950	G. Richards (201)
1949	G. Richards (261)
1948	G .Richards (224)
1947	G. Richards (269)
1946	G. Richards (212)
1945	G. Richards (104)

BOOKIES SHELL OUT ON DETTORI

Jockey Frankie Dettori's popularity coupled with Authorized's outstanding form resulted in bookmakers paying out £40 million to winning punters after the dream pair's victory in the 2007 Derby.

CHAMPION JUMP JOCKEYS 1945–2008

(No. of winners in parentheses)

2007–08	A.P. McCoy (140)
2006–07	A.P. McCoy (184)
2005–06	A.P. McCoy (178)
2004–05	A.P. McCoy (200)
2003–04	A.P. McCoy (209)
2002–03	A.P. McCoy (256)
2001–02	A.P. McCoy (289)
2000–01	A.P. McCoy (191)
1999–00	A.P. McCoy (245)
1998–99	A.P. McCoy (186)
1997–98	A.P. McCoy (253)
1996–97	A.P. McCoy (190)
1995–96	A.P. McCoy (175)
1994–95	R. Dunwoody (160)
1993–94	R. Dunwoody (197)
1992–93	R. Dunwoody (173)
1991–92	P. Scudamore (175)
1990–91	P. Scudamore (141)
1989–90	P. Scudamore (170)
1988–89	P. Scudamore (221)
1987–88	P. Scudamore (132)
1986–87	P. Scudamore (123)
1985–86	P. Scudamore (91)
1984–85	J. Francome (101)
1983–84	J. Francome (131)
1982–83	J. Francome (106)
1981–82	J. Francome (120)
	P. Scudamore (120)
1980–81	J. Francome (105)
1979–80	J.J. O'Neill (115)
1978–79	J. Francome (95)
1977–78	J.J. O'Neill (149)
1976–77	T. Stack (97)
1975–76	J Francome (96)
1974–75	T. Stack (82)
1973–74	R. Barry (94)
1972–73	R. Barry (125)
1971–72	B.R. Davies (89)
1970–71	G. Thorner (74)
1969–70	B.R. Davies (91)
1968–69	B.R. Davies (77)
	T. Biddlecombe (77)
1967–68	J. Gifford (82)
1966–67	J. Gifford (122)
1965–66	T. Biddlecombe (102)
1964–65	T. Biddlecombe (114)
1963–64	J. Gifford (94)
1962–63	J. Gifford (70)
1961–62	S. Mellor (80)
1960–61	S. Mellor (118)
1959–60	S. Mellor (68)
1958–59	T. Brookshaw (83)
1957–58	F. Winter (82)
1956–57	F. Winter (80)
1955–56	F. Winter (74)
1954–55	T. Molony (67)
1953–54	R. Francis (76)
1952–53	F. Winter (121)
1951–52	T. Molony (99)
1950–51	T. Molony (83)
1949–50	T. Molony (95)
1948–49	T. Molony (60)
1947–48	B. Marshall (66)
1946–47	J. Dowdeswell (58)
1945–46	T.F. Rimell (54)
1944–45	H. Nicholson (15)
	T.F. Rimell (15)

RACING JARGON (31)

Conditional – a young jockey tied by contract to a licensed trainer while learning the business of jump riding

FROM THE HORSE'S MOUTH (17)

"I always remember walking around the racecourse on Derby day and feeling as if I was walking on cushioned air as there is such a big atmosphere, so winning it was an unbelievable thrill!"
***Willie Carson**, reflecting on his Derby experiences*

HE GAVE US HIS HEART

The following is inscribed on the plinth beneath the statue of the legendary Mill Reef at the National Stud, Newmarket.

Swift as a bird I flew down many a course.
Princes, Lords, Commoners all sang my praise.
In victory or defeat I played my part.
Remember me, all men who love the Horse,
If hearts and spirits flag in after days;
Though small, I gave my all. I gave my heart.

RACING JARGON (32)

Stewards – these are amateur, unpaid officials attending the racecourse on behalf of the British Horseracing Authority (BHA) to ensure that the Rules of Racing are strictly adhered to.

STRONG FAMILY TIES

Richard Hannon has trained three winners of the 2000 Guineas: Mon Fils (1973), Don't Forget Me (1987) and Tirol (1990). The Hannon family has a rich horse-racing tradition – his father was a trainer, his son Richard is his assistant trainer and his son-in-law, Richard Hughes, is the stable's jockey.

FIRST NATIONAL WINNER

In 1836 The Duke, ridden by Captain Martin Becher, won the first Grand Liverpool Steeplechase at Aintree. For years it was believed that from 1836 to 1838 the most famous steeplechase in the world had not been at Aintree, but at Maghull. However, in the last 20 years horse racing historians have found indisputable evidence that the races had been staged at Aintree, though the obstacles were different. Aintree's own roll of honour credits Lottery, ridden by Jem Mason, as the first Grand National winner and that was in 1839.

PRINCELY SONG

As a result of his well-publicized romances, racehorse owner Prince Aly Khan was mentioned in a verse of Noël Coward's new 1950s lyrics for the 1928 song by Cole Porter entitled "Let's Fall in Love". Coward penned these lines:

Monkeys whenever you look do it,
Aly Khan and King Farouk do it
Let's do it, let's fall in love.

RACE OF THE CENTURY

In 1974 Bustino, ridden by Joe Mercer, trained by Major Dick Hern and owned by Lady Beaverbrook, won the St Leger. On 26 July 1975, in the King George VI and Queen Elizabeth Stakes at Ascot, Bustino found himself up against Grundy, winner of the that year's Epsom and Irish Derbies. The race has been dubbed "Britain's Race of the Century". Other runners in the race included Star Appeal, winner of the 1975 Eclipse Stakes, and one of the greatest fillies the world has ever seen, Dahlia, who was going for her third consecutive win in the race.

Major Hern put two of BustinO's stablemates, Kinglet and Highest, in the field to act as pacemakers in an attempt to tire Grundy. At the top of the straight, with half a mile of the 12-furlong race still to go, Mercer guided Bustino into the lead and quickly moved 4 lengths clear of Pat Eddery aboard Grundy. As they passed the 1 furlong pole, Grundy caught and passed Bustino. But Bustino fought back and recaptured the lead, before Grundy again moved his nose in front 50 yards from the finish line and held on for a glorious victory by half a length, with Dahlia a further 5 lengths back in third place. Grundy's winning time of 2m 26.98s annihilated the race record. Grundy ran only once more, without success, while Bustino was retired after giving everything he had. Disappointingly, at stud Grundy was not a particularly successful sire.

AINTREE TURFED

Despite Aintree hosting the Grand National since its first running in 1836, the racecourse was not actually completely turfed until 1885. Until then the area beyond the Melling Road was farmland, and during the race the horses jumped over hedges from one field to another, sometimes with a considerable drop on the other side.

SECRETARIAT

Secretariat was foaled on 30 March 1970 at Christopher Chenery's Meadow Stables in Virginia, USA, sired by Bold Ruler out of Somethingroyal. He was owned by Penny Chenery and trained by Canadian Lucien Laurin. A striking chestnut with three white socks and a star with a narrow blaze, he was unnamed as a yearling. Elizabeth Ham, the secretary at the Meadow Stables, had 10 names rejected by the Jockey Club before her choice, Secretariat, was approved. On 4 July 1972, he finished second in his first outing as a two-year-old but won his next race just 11 days later at Aqueduct.

He won his next four races, including three prestigious Stakes races: the Sanford and Hopeful at Saratoga, and Futurity at Belmont Park. It was at the Saratoga meeting that Laurin replaced apprentice Paul Feliciano with the journeyman Ron Turcotte. Secretariat then ran in the Champagne Stakes at Belmont Park. He won but was subsequently disqualified and placed second for interfering with Stop the Music. He closed out his two-year-old season defeating Stop the Music by eight lengths in the Laurel Futurity and winning the Garden State Futurity. Secretariat was named 1972 Horse of the Year, only the third two-year-old to win the honour.

Laurin knew he had a special horse and Secretariat began his three-year-old season with an easy victory in the Bay Shore Stakes before equalling the track record over 7 furlongs in the Gotham Stakes at Aqueduct. Secretariat won the 1973 Kentucky Derby at Churchill Downs in a new track record time of 1:59.40 (the time still stands today), running each quarter-mile segment faster than the previous one. Next up in his quest to land the coveted US Triple Crown was the 1³/16-mile Preakness Stakes at Pimlico. Secretariat broke last but with 5½ furlongs to the finish he ran away from the chasing pack to win by 2½ lengths in 1:53.40, a new track record.

When he landed the 1973 Belmont Stakes Secretariat became the first US Triple Crown winner in 25 years and only the ninth in history. So dominant was he in the race that he won it by 31 lengths and ran the fastest ever 1½ miles on dirt in history, 2.24, equating to 37½ miles per hour. His career record stood at 16 wins from 21 starts, with earnings of $1,316,808. He retired to stud and died on 4 October 1989, when it was discovered that his healthy heart was twice the normal size.

Did You Know That?
Secretariat was on the cover of three national magazines – *Newsweek*, *Time* and *Sportsweek* – in the lead-up to the 1973 Belmont Stakes.

THREE DECADES OF THE DERBY

Pat Eddery rode Derby winners in three different decades – Grundy in 1975, Golden Fleece in 1982 and Quest For Fame in 1990. Coincidentally, Eddery also rode his first career winner, Alvaro, at Epsom in April 1969.

HEADGEAR

Horses wearing blinkers, cheek-pieces or visors have a poor record in the Grand National. Since L'Escargot in 1975, only Earth Summit (1991) and Comply or Die (2008) have successfully carried headgear to Aintree National glory.

RACING JARGON (33)

Tote – this is the only company in Britain that is licensed to offer pool betting on racecourses. The Tote also offers a range of bets such as Exacta, Scoop6, Jackpot and Placepot.

LEGAL DRUGS

In 1968 Dancer's Image, ridden by Bobby Ussery and trained by Lou Cavalaris Jr, finished first in the Kentucky Derby but was subsequently disqualified after a post-race urine sample revealed traces of the banned drug Phenylbutazone in the horse. Phenylbutazone – better known as bute – is now legal for use on racehorses in many US states, including Kentucky.

STEWART BREAKS HIS FESTIVAL DUCK

Celestial Halo's win in the 2008 JCB Triumph Hurdle at the Cheltenham Festival with Ruby Walsh in the saddle broke owner Andy Stewart's nine-year duck at the festival.

A DOUBLE HENNESSY

In 1960 Derek Ancil rode and trained Knucklecracker to win the Hennessy Cognac Gold Cup. Since then, two jockeys have ridden and subsequently trained Hennessy winners: Andy Turnell partnered April Seventh in 1975 and trained Cogent in 1993 and Paul Nicholls rode Broadheath in 1986 and Playschool (1987), before sending out Strong Flow (2003) and Denman (2007).

FROM THE HORSE'S MOUTH (18)

"In racing there's nothing more exciting than winning a race by a short head. I'd rather win in a photo finish than by three lengths. At the same time, the biggest turn-off is losing by a head. Then I'd rather be last. You know there will be people saying that the horse would have won if a lad had been on board."
Hayley Turner

IRISH–ENGLISH NATIONAL DOUBLE

The Irish Grand National at Fairyhouse has a poor record for providing Grand National winners. Only three horses, Numbersixvalverde (Fairyhouse in 2005, Aintree 2006), Bobbyjo (Fairyhouse 1998, Aintree 1999) and Rhyme 'N' Reason (Fairyhouse 1985, Aintree 1988), have managed to complete a National double since 1945.

GLASS SLIPPER TURNS GOLD

In 1980 Light Cavalry, ridden by Joe Mercer, trained by Henry Cecil and owned by Jim Joel, won the St Leger. The following year Fairy Footsteps, ridden by Lester Piggott, trained by Henry Cecil and owned by Jim Joel, won the 1000 Guineas. Both Classic winners were out of Glass Slipper, Light Cavalry sired by Brigadier Gerard and Fairy Footsteps sired by the legendary Mill Reef.

CHAMPION QUEEN

When Carrozza, ridden by Lester Piggott and trained by Noel Murless, landed the Oaks in 1957 it helped her owner, Queen Elizabeth II, to become the Champion Flat Owner that year. It was the Queen's first Classic winner. She was also the Champion Flat Owner in 1954.

HENNESSY COGNAC GOLD CUP

The Hennessy Cognac Gold Cup Handicap Chase is the longest continuously sponsored race in Britain. Run in late November or early December, it was first run at Newbury in 1960 after three years at Cheltenham. The Grade 3 steeplechase is run over 3 miles 2½ furlongs with 21 fences to be jumped. Among the great horses to have won the race are: Arkle, Bregawn, Burrough Hill Lad, Denman, Kerstin, Mandarin and Mill House (all also landed the Cheltenham Gold Cup).

FRED WINTER

Frederick Thomas Winter was born on 20 September 1926 in Andover, Hampshire, the son of a jockey, also Fred (who had won the 1911 Oaks on Cherimoya as a 16-year-old). Young Fred started riding his father's horses at their Surrey stable when he was just five years old, becoming a successful gymkhana rider. At 13 and weighing 5st 7lb, he had his first public ride at Newbury on Tam O'Shanter. They finished ninth in a field of 21, but Tam O'Shanter gave Fred his first winner following eight rides at Salisbury.

Shortly after his maiden victory he left school to join Henri Jellis as an apprentice at his Newmarket stable. However, Winter was not successful at Jellis's yard, riding just two winners in 80 starts while his body weight was rapidly rising. Winter left Newmarket and teamed up with his father at Southfleet while at the same time enlisting in the army for four years. He was demobbed in 1948.

The year before he left the army he was on leave and he decided that his future lay in steeplechasing, and he had his first outing as a jump jockey on his father's Bambino II, coming in fifth. The very next day he landed his first win over hurdles on another of his dad's horses, Carlton. Following an injury, which kept him out of action for a year, he rode 18 winners from 131 rides in season 1949–50. In 1951–52 Winter finished runner-up to champion jockey Tim Molony, claiming 84 winners. However, the following season he won the first of his four Champion Jockey titles and he did so in style, riding 121 winners, a record that would stand for 14 seasons.

In addition to his four Jockeys' Championships (he also took the title in 1955–56, 1956–57 and 1957–58) he won the Grand National twice (on Sundew and Kilmore), the Champion Hurdle three times (aboard Clair Soleil, Fare Time and Eborneezer) and two Cheltenham Gold Cups (riding Saffron Tartan and Mandarin).

Winter retired as a jockey in 1964, having ridden a then record 923 National Hunt winners, and turned his attention to training. He was the leading National Hunt trainer eight times between 1971 and 1985, won the Grand National twice (with Jay Trump and Anglo), the Cheltenham Gold Cup (Midnight Court), three Champion Hurdles (Bula, Lanzarote and Celtic Shot) and a Champion Chase (Crisp). He retired from training in 1988, following a stroke, and died on 5 April 2004.

Did You Know That?
Fred Winter is the only man ever to win the Cheltenham Gold Cup, Grand National and Champion Hurdle as a trainer and as a jockey.

ARC DE TRIOMPHE WINNERS 1946–2008

Year	*Winner*	*Jockey*	*Trainer*
2008	Zarkava	C. Soumillon	A. de Royer-Dupre
2007	Dylan Thomas	K. Fallon	A.P. O'Brien
2006	Rail Link	S. Pasquier	A. Fabre
2005	Hurricane Run	K. Fallon	A. Fabre
2004	Bago	T. Gillet	J. Pease
2003	Dalakhani	S. Soumillon	A. de Royer-Dupre
2002	Marienbard	L. Dettori	S. Bin Suroor
2001	Sahkee	L. Dettori	S. Bin Suroor
2000	Sinndar	J. Murtagh	J. Oxx
1999	Montjeu	M. Kinane	J. Hammond
1998	Sagamix	O. Peslier	A. Fabre
1997	Peintre Célèbre	O. Peslier	A. Fabre
1996	Helissio	O. Peslier	E. Lellouche
1995	Lammtarra	L. Dettori	S. Bin Suroor
1994	Carnegie	T. Jarnet	A. Fabre
1993	Urban Sea	E. Saint-Martin	J. Lesbordes
1992	Subotica	T. Jarnet	A. Fabre
1991	Suave Dancer	C. Asmussen	J. Hammond
1990	Saumarez	G. Mosse	N. Clement
1989	Carroll House	M. Kinane	M. Jarvis
1988	Tony Bin	J. Reid	L. Camici
1987	Trempolino	P. Eddery	A. Fabre
1986	Dancing Brave	P. Eddery	G. Harwood
1985	Rainbow Quest	P. Eddery	J. Tree
1984	Sagace	Y. Saint-Martin	P.L. Biancone
1983	All Along	W.R. Swinburn	P.L. Biancone
1982	Akiyda	Y. Saint-Martin	F. Mathet
1981	Gold River	G. Moore Jr	A. Head
1980	Detroit	P. Eddery	O. Douieb
1979	Three Troikas	F. Head	C. Head
1978	Alleged	L. Piggott	M.V. O'Brien
1977	Alleged	L. Piggott	M.V. O'Brien
1976	Ivanjica	F. Head	A. Head
1975	Star Appeal	G. Starkey	T. Grieper
1974	Allez France	Y Saint-Martin	A. Penna Sr
1973	Rheingold	L. Piggott	B. Hills
1972	San San	F. Head	A. Penna Sr
1971	Mill Reef	G. Lewis	I. Balding
1970	Sassafras	Y. Saint-Martin	F. Mathet
1969	Lev Moss	W. Williamson	S. McGrath

1968	Vaguely Noble	W. Williamson	E. Pollet
1967	Topyo	W. Pyers	C. Bartholomew
1966	Bon Mot III	F. Head	W. Head
1965	Sea-Bird II	P. Glennon	E. Pollet
1964	Prince Royal II	R. Poincelet	G. Bridgland
1963	Exbury	J. Deforge	G. Watson
1962	Soltikoff	M. Depalmas	R. Pelat
1961	Molvedo	E. Camici	A. Maggi
1960	Puissant Chef	M. Garcia	C. Bartholomew
1959	Saint Crespin*	G. Moore	A. Head
1958	Ballymoss	A. Breasley	M.V. O'Brien
1957	Oroso	S. Boullenger	D. Lescalle
1956	Ribot	E. Camici	U. Penco
1955	Ribot	E. Camici	I. Della Rocchetta
1954	Sica Boy	W.R. Johnstone	P. Pelat
1953	La Sorellina	M. Larraun	E. Pollet
1952	Nuccio	R. Poincelet	A. Head
1951	Tantieme	J. Doyasbère	F. Mathet
1950	Tantieme	J. Doyasbère	F. Mathet
1949	Coronation	R. Poincelet	C. Semblat
1948	Migoli	C. Smirke	F. Butters
1947	La Paillon	F. Rochetti	W. Head
1946	Caracella	C. Elliott	C. Semblat

* *Midnight Sun dead-heated but was disqualified.*

WHEN THE WINNER FINISHED SECOND

In the 1973 Cheltenham Gold Cup Pendil was the odds-on favourite to win the race and looked so dominant approaching the last fence with Richard Pitman at the controls that the legendary BBC TV commentator Sir Peter O'Sullevan declared him the winner. However, to the dismay of the crowd and the television viewers watching at home The Dikler, ridden by Ron Barry, caught and passed Pendil on the run-in. In 1974 Pendil (with Pitman in the saddle again) was once again the odds-on favourite to win the race but was brought down with three fences to jump.

UNDER WATCHFUL EYE

The American thoroughbred stallion Storm Cat commanded a stud fee of £250,000 ($500,000) in 2007 and is one of the few horses in the world who has a 24-hour armed guard watching over him.

DERBY–2000 GUINEAS DOUBLES

Ten horses have completed the Derby–2000 Guineas double since 1919. Bahram and Nijinsky also won the St Leger to take the Triple Crown.

1925	Manna
1931	Cameronian
1935	Bahram
1939	Blue Peter
1949	Nimbus
1957	Crepello
1967	Royal Palace
1968	Sir Ivor
1970	Nijinsky
1989	Nashwan

RACING JARGON (34)

Judge – this is the official employed by the British Horseracing Authority (BHA) to declare the finishing order of a race and the distances between the runners.

DUNLOP'S 10 CLASSICS

John L. Dunlop was one of Britain's leading trainers, saddling over 3,000 winners between 1966 and 2002. In 1995 Dunlop was British Champion Trainer and he trained 10 English Classic winners:

1000 Guineas:	Quick as Lightning 1980, Salsabil 1990, Shadayid 1991
Derby:	Shirley Heights 1978, Erhaab 1994
Oaks:	Circus Plume 1984, Salsabil 1990
St Leger:	Moon Madness 1986, Silver Patriarch 1997, Millenary 2000

John Dunlop's son, Ed, trained the winner of the 2004 Oaks, Ouija Board.

QUEEN MOTHER YOUNG AND OLD

In 1977 Skymas became the oldest horse to land the Queen Mother Champion Chase at Cheltenham, aged 12. The 2008 winner, Master Minded, became the youngest ever winner aged just five.

MISTAKE WINS THE DERBY

Ireland's New Approach won the 2008 Derby with his owner admitting after the race that he had been left in the Classic by mistake. His win gave a trio their first ever success in the race – jockey Kevin Manning, trainer Jim Bolger and owner Princess Haya of Jordan. The princess was given the horse as a present by her husband, His Highness Sheikh Mohammed bin Rashid Al Maktoum. Meanwhile, Sheikh Mohammed was still waiting for one of his Godolphin horses to win the Classic in his silks.

New Approach, the leading two-year-old in 2007 who had finished second to Henrythenavigator in both the English and Irish 2000 Guineas in 2008, strode to an impressive victory in the blue riband of flat racing. Bolger had always maintained that he wasn't keen to run the horse in the Derby but mistakenly forgot to remove his name from the list of entries earlier in the year. "It's the biggest mistake I ever made in my life. However, it's turned out to be a fortuitous one, but I gladly admit that it was a mistake. I am delighted. Before the race I thought winning it would be up there with the other special ones but I have to say having now won it this is very special," said a delighted Bolger. For Manning, Bolger's son-in-law, New Approach was only his second ride in the Epsom classic.

NATIONAL LUCK OF THE IRISH

Since the late 1990s Irish-bred horses have enjoyed great success in the Grand National. Horses foaled in Ireland won seven times between 1999 and 2008. In fact, Irish runners finished first, second and fourth in 2006 and first and third in 2007. In 2008 Irish-bred horses filled the first five places, with Comply or Die the winner. In addition the five jockeys also were born in Ireland:

	Horse	*Trainer*	*Jockey*
1	Comply Or Die	D.E. Pipe	Timmy Murphy
2	King Johns Castle	A.L.T. Moore	P. Carberry
3	Snowy Morning	W.P. Mullins	D.J. Casey
4	Slim Pickings	T.J. Taaffe	B.J. Geraghty
5	Bewleys Berry	J. Howard Johnson	Denis O'Regan

NOT MUCH VALUE TO BE HAD

Arkle won the 1966 Cheltenham Gold Cup at odds of 1-10, the shortest-priced winner of the race ever.

FROM THE HORSE'S MOUTH (19)

"I'm choked. It's been physically and mentally draining over the past month. This was the best result that could have happened for racing as no one deserved to lose. He [Seb Sanders] is the toughest rival you could ever meet."
***Jamie Spencer**, talking about his shared Champion Jockey title in 2007*

LEGENDARY IRISH NATIONAL WINNERS

Arkle won the Irish Grand National in 1964, and another legend, Desert Orchid, won it in 1990.

KING OF KINGS TOPS FRENCH KING

In 1998 the Irish-bred and trained King of Kings, ridden by Michael Kinane, trained by Aidan O'Brien and owned by Michael Tabor and Sue Magnier, beat the French 10-11 favourite Xaar (Europe's champion two-year-old) to land the 2000 Guineas. King of Kings was the 28-year-old O'Brien's first English Classic runner but, sadly, the horse was injured running in the Derby and was retired to stud.

Did You Know That?
Seven weeks before King of Kings won at Newmarket, O'Brien had guided Istabraq to the first of his three Champion Hurdle victories

THE STAYERS' TRIPLE CROWN

The Ascot Gold Cup, Doncaster Cup and Goodwood Cup form Britain's Stayers' Triple Crown for horses capable of running longer distances. Only six horses have ever landed this unique treble, while Le Moss is the only horse to do it twice.

CHELTENHAM GOLD CUP HAT-TRICK

The Henrietta Knight-trained Best Mate is the most successful winner of the Gold Cup in recent times, claiming victory with Jim Culloty in the saddle in 2002, 2003 and 2004.

NORTH AMERICAN BORDER RAIDS

Only two Canadian-bred horses have won the Kentucky Derby – Northern Dancer in 1964 and Sunny's Halo in 1983.

GATWICK NATIONALS

For three years during the First World War Aintree was closed for racing, the War Office having taken it over, and therefore an alternative race to the Aintree Grand National was run at Gatwick Racecourse. The 1916 race was called "The Racecourse Association Steeplechase" and the following two were known as "The War National Steeplechase". However, some historians do not recognize these three war races as "Grand Nationals". Gatwick was opened in 1891 and hosted races until it closed in 1940. Gatwick Airport was built on the racecourse site in 1950.

A CLASSIC QUAD

In 1996 John Gosden trained the first of his four Classic winners when Shantou won the St Leger. His second, and greatest, came at Epsom Downs the following year when Benny The Dip landed the Derby. In 2000 Lahan claimed the 2000 Guineas and in 2007 Lucarno won him his second St Leger.

THE STUDS

At the end of the 2007 flat racing season, Dylan Thomas retired from racing and started a new life at stud. The 2007 winner of the King George VI and Queen Elizabeth Diamond Stakes, Prix Ganay, Irish Champion Stakes and the Prix de l'Arc de Triomphe was sent to the Coolmore Stud, where he commanded a stud fee of €35,000. The pride of the Ballydoyle Stable was the most expensive of the new stallions standing in 2008 and and fifth dearest of all horses standing. Another of the Coolmore stallions was 14-time champion sire Sadler's Wells.

Three other top horses who beat Dylan Thomas in 2007 were also retired to stud: Notnowcato, who won the Tattersalls Gold Cup at The Curragh, went to Stanley House at Newmarket where he commanded a fee of £8,000; the winner of Royal Ascot's Prince of Wales Stakes, Manduro, will cover a mare at Dalham Hall Stud in Newmarket for £20,000; and the York International Stakes (and Derby) winner, Authorized, was sent to stand at Kildangan in County Kildare, with a stud fee of €25,000. The first crop of foals will appear in 2009 but they won't race in public until 2011.

Dylan Thomas won 10 of his 19 races, including six Group 1s, and earned £3.38 million in prize money. To earn the same money again, Dylan Thomas will need to cover around 115 mares, something some stallions can achieve in a single year!

LESTER AND WILLIE

After Lester Piggott, Willie Carson is the only jockey in the Derby's illustrious history to have won the world's most famous flat race more than three times. Piggott won it nine times, Carson four.

THE HORSE WHO LOVED CHEESE

Brown Jack, the legendary steeplechaser from the 1930s, enjoyed a devoted following of fans who regularly sent him his favourite food – cheese. After his racing days were over Brown Jack was immortalized in the Philip Larkin poem "At Grass".

THE QUEEN MOTHER AND LESTER

Brian Harding's win on One Man in the 1998 Queen Mother Champion Chase earned him the Lester Award for Jump Ride of the Year.

IN THE COURT OF KING ANDRE

In 1991 the French trainer André Fabre won his first English Classic, the St Leger, with Toulon (ridden by Pat Eddery and owned by Khalid Abdullah). Two years later he won the Oaks with Intrepidity (ridden by Michael Roberts and owned by Sheikh Mohammed) plus the 2000 Guineas with Zafonic (ridden by Pat Eddery and owned by Khalid Abdullah). His fourth and final Classic in England came in 1995 when Pennekamp (ridden by Thierry Jamet and owned by Sheikh Mohammed) won the 2000 Guineas.

Fabre is a highly successful trainer, particularly in France where he has won the Prix de l'Arc de Triomphe seven times: Trempolino (1987), Subotica (1992), Carnegie (1994), Peintre Celebre (1997), Sagamix (1998), Hurricane Run (2005) and Rail Link (2006); the Grand Prix de Paris nine times: Dancehall (1989), Subotica (1991), Homme de Loi (1992), Fort Wood (1993), Grape Tree Road (1996), Peintre Celebre (1997), Limpid (1998), Slickly (1999) and Rail Link (2006); and the French equivalent of the Derby, the Prix du Jockey Club, with Peintre Celebre in 1997. Along with John Cunnington (Le Pacha, 1941) he is the only man to have trained the winner of the French Triple Crown. André has been the leading trainer in France for the past 19 years (1989–2007). In 2005 (with Hurricane Run, winner of the 2006 King George VI and Queen Elizabeth Diamond Stakes) and 2007 (with Manduro) he trained the number one rated racehorse in the world.

SIR MICHAEL STOUTE

In 1972 Michael Ronald Stoute began his career training horses at Newmarket, having arrived in England from Barbados a few years earlier. In 1978 he landed his first Classic victory, the Oaks, with Fair Salinia, ridden by Greville Starkey (owned by Sven Hanson). Stoute never looked back and added 20 more Classics (English and Irish) in addition to prestigious races away from British shores, most notably the Breeders' Cup (Pilsudski 1996, Kalanisi 2000) and the Dubai World Cup (Singspiel 1997).

In 1990, after 18 years training many flat winners, Stoute switched racing codes and trained the winner of the Champion Hurdle in 1990, Kribensis. His dual training role has since produced many exceptional horses at his Freemason Lodge Stables, with many believing that the legendary Shergar was without question his greatest achievement. Stoute, who can boast Queen Elizabeth II among his long list of owners, was knighted in 1998 for services to tourism in his native Barbados.

Did You Know That?
Sir Michael Stoute was the only trainer in the 20th century to win a Classic in five successive seasons (1985–89), but the St Leger has somehow managed to elude his grasp.

BONUS MISS

If Kauto Star had won the 2008 Cheltenham Gold Cup his owner, Clive D. Smith, would have collected a £1 million bonus for winning the Betfair Chase, King George VI Chase and Cheltenham Gold Cup in the same season. He was beaten by his stable-companion Denman.

RACING JARGON (35)

Clerk of the scales – this is the official employed by the British Horseracing Authority (BHA) to ensure all horses carry the correct weight for each race. The jockeys are weighed in and weighed out before and after each race.

MASTER MINDED

Master Minded won the 2008 Queen Mother Champion Chase after seeing off the challenge of the 2007 winner, Voy Por Ustedes, by 19 lengths at the Cheltenham Festival.

RACING ROUND AINTREE

In addition to horse racing, Aintree has also hosted five British Formula 1 motor racing Grands Prix and a European Grand Prix. Sir Stirling Moss won his first Grand Prix in Liverpool in 1955.

INGLIS DREVER'S FESTIVAL HISTORY

In 2008 Inglis Drever, ridden by Denis O'Regan, made Cheltenham Festival history by edging out Kasbah Bliss at the line to claim his third World Hurdle victory. The 11-8 favourite trained by Howard Johnson followed up on his wins in 2005 and 2007.

RACING SCANDALS (10)

Between 1910 and 1920 the notorious trainer Peter "Ringer" Barrie used to paint horses different colours using henna dyes so as to fix the outcome of a race (he also gave some horses new identities). However, his activities soon caught up with him and he was brought to trial. At his trial the judge asked Barrie what his definition of "a good thing" was. Barrie smiled and replied, "A good three-year-old in a bad two-year-old race." When he was banned from racing in Britain he switched his attention to the USA, Canada, Cuba and Mexico, where he continued to change a chestnut to a bay and vice versa. Because of Barrie's cheating, racing introduced a number of measures in order to help improve racehorse identification. One of these measures was lip tattooing, but this was only introduced in North America; the Jockey Club insisted that such "drastic measures" would not be necessary.

NOTHING TO LAUGH ABOUT

In 1953 Happy Laughter, ridden by Manny Mercer, the brother of fellow jockey Joe, trained by Jack Jarvis and owned by David Will, won the 1000 Guineas. Sadly Manny was killed in September 1959 at an Ascot meeting. He was riding Priddy Fair down to the start when the animal reared up and threw Manny against the rails. The horse kicked Manny in the head and he died immediately on the Ascot turf. As a mark of respect racing was abandoned for the day.

HORSE OF THE MILLENNIUM

In a poll in 2000, readers of the *Sun* newspaper voted the 1970 Triple Crown winner Nijinsky their "Horse of the Millennium".

NEARCO

Nearco was an Italian-bred (by Federico Tesio) racehorse foaled in 1935. Sired by Pharos out of Nogara, he was one of the most important sires of the 20th century. Nearco won all seven of his outings as a two-year-old, including the 1937 Italian Gran Criterium. A year later he was equally invincible, winning the Italian 2000 Guineas by 6 lengths and the Italian Derby by a distance, before going on to win the Gran Premio d'Italia and the Grand Premio di Milano. In the 1938 Grand Prix de Paris, run over 1 mile 7 furlongs, he moved into the lead early in the straight and left the field scrapping for second place.

He retired undefeated after the 1938 season, having won all 14 of his races and amassed $86,328 in prize money. But amid the political turmoil and the likelihood of a second world war, Tesio sold Nearco for £60,000 (a world record sum paid for a sire at the time) to Martin H. Benson of Beech House Stud at Newmarket. Nearco became an outstandingly prepotent sire, eclipsed only by his grandson, Northern Dancer, the father of the legendary Nijinsky. Nearco's progeny included Dante (winner of the 1945 Derby) and Nimbus (winner of the Derby and 2000 Guineas in 1949). From his daughters, Nearco was the damsire of the French multiple Group 1 winner Charlottesville and of the 1948 Derby winner Arctic Prince.

His male line descendants included Arkle (Cheltenham Gold Cup winner in 1964, 1965, 1966), Ballymoss (winner of the 1957 St Leger and 1958 Prix de l'Arc de Triomphe), Invasor (Uruguyan Triple Crown winner in 2005 and winner of the 2006 Breeders' Cup Classic), Never Say Die (winner of the 1958 Derby and St Leger), Shergar (1981 Derby winner), Sir Ivor (winner of the 2000 Guineas and Derby in 1968), Mill Reef (winner of the Derby and Prix de l'Arc de Triomphe in 1971), Roberto (1972 Derby winner), Secretariat (winner of the US Triple Crown in 1973), The Minstrel (1977 Derby winner) and Shirley Heights (1978 Derby winner). According to France Galop, the governing body of flat and steeplechase horse racing in France, the male bloodline of every Prix de l'Arc de Triomphe winner from 1994 to 2007 could be attributed to Nearco, who was also the leading sire in Great Britain and Ireland in 1947 and 1949.

Nearco died on 27 June 1957 and was buried at Beech House Stud at Newmarket.

Did You Know That?

Tesio, as well as breeding and owning Nearco, was also the colt's trainer. He trained the winner of 21 Derbies around Europe.

FROM THE HORSE'S MOUTH (20)

"My family, who are not racing people, have been watching this rather than *Coronation Street* or *EastEnders*. It caught the imagination of everybody."
Seb Sanders*, on the exciting climax to the 2007 season*

DERBY DAY MOVED

In 1995 the Derby was run for the first time since 1953 on a Saturday after being switched from its traditional Wednesday date. The 14-1 outsider Lammtarra, ridden by Walter Swinburn – his third and final Derby winner – took the spoils in a new record time (Swinburn also won in 1981 on Shergar and in 1986 on Shahrastani). Lammtarra was also the first horse to win the Derby on his seasonal debut since Grand Parade in 1919. Quite amazingly, Shaamit equalled this feat in 1996.

Lammtarra also won the King George VI and Queen Elizabeth Diamond Stakes and the Prix de l'Arc de Triomphe in that same year. Sired by the legendary Nijinsky, Lammtarra won all four races he entered, with his first win coming in the 1994 Washington Singer Stakes. Frankie Dettori, who rode Lammtarra to victory in the King George and the Arc, said he was "possibly" the best horse he'd ever ridden. "Maybe Lammtarra is the best, because he remained unbeaten," said Dettori. Lammtarra was sold to a group of Japanese breeders for $30 million in 1996 and initially commanded a stud fee of £30,000. In 2006 Lammtarra was purchased by Sheikh Mohammed and he stands at his Dalham House Stud in Newmarket.

UNIQUE NATIONAL QUAD

Ruby Walsh is the only jockey in modern times to have won all four Grand Nationals – English, Irish, Scottish and Welsh.

WELD WEAVES HIS MAGIC

Dermot Weld trained the 1981 Oaks winner, Blue Wind, and is the only European trainer to have saddled the winner of the Melbourne Cup in Australia, a feat he achieved twice, with Vintage Crop in 1993 and Media Puzzle in 2002. Vintage Crop also won the Irish St Leger in 1993 and 1994 and the Curragh Cup in 1993 and 1995. Weld is also the only Europe-based trainer to win a leg of the American Triple Crown, Go And Go winning the 1990 Belmont Stakes.

GRANDAD WINS THE 2000 GUINEAS

When Lester Piggott won his 30th and final English Classic, the 2000 Guineas in 1992 aboard Rodrigo de Triano, he was a 56-year-old grandfather.

AN IRISH LEGEND

In 1920 Tetratema (1917–39), ridden by Brownie Carslake, trained by Atty Persse and owned and bred by Major Dermot McAlmont, cruised to victory in the 2000 Guineas. Aged two Tetratema won all of his races and was the leading stakes winner in 1919 ahead of older horses – National Breeders Produce Stakes, Molecomb Stakes, Middle Park Stakes, Imperial Produce Plate and Champagne Stakes. As a three-year-old in 1920 he was just as successful, winning the Fern Hill Stakes, Kennett Stakes, 2000 Guineas and the King George Stakes. Aged four he was the undefeated Champion Sprinter, winning the King's Stand Stakes, King George Stakes, Snailwell Stakes and July Cup. Following his July Cup victory he was retired to stand at stud at his owner's Ballylinch Stud, Thomastown, County Kilkenny, Ireland.

In 1929 he was the leading sire in Great Britain and Ireland and his progeny included: Mr Jinks, winner of the 2000 Guineas in 1929; Royal Minstrel, winner of the 1929 Eclipse Stakes; Fourth Hand, winner of the 1927 Irish 2000 Guineas, and Four Course, winner of the 1000 Guineas in 1931, and champion two-year-olds Foray II and filly Myrobella,. He died in 1939 and was buried at Ballylinch Stud near his sire, The Tetrarch, and his son, Mr Jinks.

Did You Know That?
The USA's National Sporting Library described The Tetrarch as "probably the greatest two-year-old of all time" and "possibly the greatest runner ever".

THE KENTUCKY–EPSOM DERBY LINK

In June 1986, Bold Arrangement, trained by Clive Brittain for Anthony and Raymond Richards, ran in the Epsom Derby, thus becoming the first horse to have also run in the Kentucky Derby. A month earlier, ridden by Chris McCarron at Churchill Downs, he ran second behind Ferdinand, but at Epsom he was a disappointing 14th of 17 in Shahrastani's race. In 1992 Dr Devious became the first Epsom Derby winner to have earlier run in the Kentucky Derby.

MELBOURNE CUP WINNERS 1946–2008

Year	*Winner*	*Jockey*	*Trainer*
2008	Viewed	Blake Shinn	Bart Cummings
2007	Efficient	Michael Rodd	Graeme Rogerson
2006	Delta Blues	Yasunari Iwata	Katsuhiko Sumii
2005	Makybe Diva	Glen Boss	Lee Freedman
2004	Makybe Diva	Glen Boss	Lee Freedman
2003	Makybe Diva	Glen Boss	David Hall
2002	Media Puzzle	Damien Oliver	Dermot K. Weld
2001	Ethereal	Scott Seamer	Sheila Laxon
2000	Brew	Kerrin McEvoy	Mike Moroney
1999	Rogan Josh	John Marshall	Bart Cummings
1998	Jezabeel	Chris Munce	Brian Jenkins
1997	Might and Power	Jim Cassidy	Jack Denham
1996	Saintly	Darren Beadman	Bart Cummings
1995	Doriemus	Damien Oliver	Lee Freedman
1994	Jeune	Wayne Harris	David Hayes
1993	Vintage Crop	Michael Kinane	Dermot K. Weld
1992	Subzero	Greg Hall	Lee Freedman
1991	Let's Elope	Steven King	Bart Cummings
1990	Kingston Rule	Darren Beadman	Bart Cummings
1989	Tawrrific	Shane Dye	Lee Freedman
1988	Empire Rose	Tony Allan	Laurie Laxon
1987	Kensei	Larry Olsen	Les J. Bridge
1986	At Talaq	Michael Clarke	C.S. Hayes
1985	What A Nuisance	Pat Hyland	John Meagher
1984	Black Knight	Pete Cook	George Hanlon
1983	Kiwi	Jim Cassidy	Ewen S. Lupton
1982	Gurner's Lane	Mick J. Dittman	Geoff T. Murphy
1981	Just A Dash	Pete Cook	T.J. Smith
1980	Beldale Ball	John Letts	C.S. Hayes
1979	Hyperno	Harry White	Bart Cummings
1978	Arwon	Harry White	George Hanlon
1977	Gold And Black	John Duggan	Bart Cummings
1976	Van Der Hum	Robert J. Skelton	Len H. Robinson
1975	Think Big	Harry White	Bart Cummings
1974	Think Big	Harry White	Bart Cummings
1973	Gala Supreme	Frank Reys	Ray J. Hutchins
1972	Piping Lane	John Letts	George Hanlon
1971	Silver Knight	R. Bruce Marsh	Eric Temperton
1970	Baghdad Note	Midge Didham	Robert Heasley
1969	Rain Lover	Jim Johnson	Mick L. Robins

Year	Winner	Jockey	Trainer
1968	Rain Lover	Jim Johnson	Mick L. Robins
1967	Red Handed	Roy Higgins	Bart Cummings
1966	Galilee	John Miller	Bart Cummings
1965	Light Fingers	Roy Higgins	Bart Cummings
1964	Polo Prince	Ron Taylor	John P. Carter
1963	Gatum Gatum	Jim Johnson	H Graham Heagney
1962	Even Stevens	Les Coles	Arch McGregor
1961	Lord Fury	Ray Selkrig	Frank B. Lewis
1960	Hi Jinx	William A. Smith	Trevor H. Knowles
1959	Macdougal	Pat Glennon	Richard W. Roden
1958	Baystone	Mel Schumacher	Jack Green
1957	Straight Draw	Noel L. McGrowdie	J.M. Mitchell
1956	Evening Peal	George Podmore	E.D. Lawson
1955	Toparoa	Neville Sellwood	T.J. Smith
1954	Rising Fast	Jack Purtell	Ivan Tucker
1953	Wodalla	Jack Purtell	Robert Sinclair
1952	Dalray	Bill Williamson	C.C. McCarthy
1951	Delta	Neville Sellwood	Maurice McCarten
1950	Comic Court	Pat Glennon	J.M. Cummings
1949	Foxzami	William Fellows	D. Lewis
1948	Rimfire	Ray Neville	Stan Boyden
1947	Hiraji	Jack Purtell	J.W. McCurley
1946	Russia	Darby Munro	E. Hush

GRAND NATIONAL'S FIRST HURDLE

Before every Grand National the build-up, parade and regirthing prior to the off lasts for approximately 25 minutes, more than double the time it takes for any other race.

OVER AND OUT

The 1997 Grand National witnessed Sir Peter O'Sullevan's 50th and final commentary on the race for the BBC. It was won by Lord Gyllene, trained by Steve Brookshaw and ridden by Tony Dobbin.

FRANCE'S ONLY GOLD CUP WIN

The Fellow was the only French-trained winner of the Cheltenham Gold Cup, trained by François Doumen and ridden to victory by Adam Kondrat in 1994.

A BLACK CAT AND THE DERBY

Prior to the running of the 1929 Derby, Lord Astor's Cragadour was the red-hot favourite to land the Classic. However, when the punters read in the newspaper that a black cat knocked over a small silver statue of the horse on display in a London shop, and then the shop was broken into and the statue stolen, the punters became nervous. The superstitious among the betting fraternity began to hedge their bets on another runner, Mr Jinks, a grey horse named by the president of Ireland, William Cosgrave.

On the day of the race the betting could not separate Cragadour, Mr Jinks and Lord Derby's runner, Hunter's Moon. However, across the Irish Sea the word on the street was that Trigo, Irish bred and Irish owned (by William Barnett), would land the Classic, resulting in many Irish punters wagering what they had in their pockets on him at generous odds of 33-1. Trigo didn't let his Irish fans down and won with Joe Marshall, an apprentice jockey, at the reins.

THE SHOE

Billie Lee "Willie" Shoemaker was born on 19 August 1931 in the west Texas town of Fabens, USA. When he was born he weighed less than 1,134 grams (40 ounces) and was 26.5 centimetres (10½ inches) long. Legend has it that his grandmother put him in a shoebox that she placed next to an oven to keep Willie alive during the first night after he was born. "The Shoe", as he was affectionately nicknamed, won 11 US Triple Crown races, 1,009 stakes races and 10 national money titles. In 1953 Shoemaker set the record for the most winners (485) in a year which was unbeaten for 20 years. In 1986 he rode Ferdinand to victory in the Kentucky Derby and at 54 years of age he became the oldest jockey to win the Run for the Roses. His last win in the saddle came on 20 January 1990 aboard Beau Genius in the Hallandale Handicap at Gulfstream Park in Florida. Exactly two weeks later he mounted a horse in a race for the 40,352nd and final time, partnering the seven-year-old Patchy Groundfog at Santa Anita. Shoemaker's career winnings amounted to a colossal $123 million. He rode 8,833 winners during his 42-year career, a world record that stood until Laffit Pincay Jr broke it in 1999.

FOOT-AND-MOUTH OUTBREAK

In 1967, the Government banned horse racing in Britain for more than a month following an outbreak of foot-and-mouth disease.

SHERGAR

Shergar was foaled in 1978, bred by his owner Prince Karim Aga Khan IV at his Ballymany Stud Farm, County Kildare, Ireland. He was sired by Great Nephew out of Sharmeen, a bay colt with a very distinctive white blaze. As a two-year-old, with Lester Piggott in the saddle, he first ran at Newbury on 19 September 1980 in a 1-mile event which he won by 2½ lengths in a new course record time.

In the spring of 1981 he was quoted at 33-1 for that year's Derby, but after easily winning his seasonal reappearance in the Guardian Classic Trial at Sandown Park by 10 lengths, followed by a 12-length Chester Vase win, he was made a red-hot favourite for the Derby. At Epsom, he obliterated the field, with 19-year-old Walter Swinburn, riding in his first Derby, taking the lead three furlongs out, and winning by 10 lengths, a record that remains unbeaten to this day. After his Epsom stroll he landed the Irish Derby by 4 lengths (ridden by Piggott) and the King George VI and Queen Elizabeth Diamond Stales (ridden by Swinburn). However, he finished fourth in his last race, the St Leger. He raced eight times in his career, winning six of them, for career earnings of $684,479. He was given a Timeform rating of 140, the fifth highest ranking ever awarded.

After landing the Epsom Classic and being named European Horse of the Year for 1981, he was retired to Ballymany Stud. The Aga Khan sold 34 shares in Shergar for £250,000 each, keeping six for himself, producing a valuation of £10 million, then a record for a stallion standing at stud in Europe.

On 8 February 1983 Shergar was kidnapped from the Ballymany Stud by masked gunmen. No one has ever claimed responsibility for his theft but the most generally accepted account of his kidnapping is that he was abducted by an IRA unit. Many sportswriters have signed up to this account of his disappearance, and it has been claimed that the IRA demanded a ransom of £2 million and when the negotiations broke down they killed the horse. Shergar's remains have never been found. The kidnapping of one of the most famous racehorses ever to grace the turf has been the inspiration for several books, documentaries and even a movie starring Mickey Rourke.

Did You Know That?
Shergar was the fourth famous racehorse to be stolen. Corrida (European Horse of the Year in 1936 and 1937) disappeared without trace in France in 1944, Carnauba in Italy in 1975 and Fanfreluche (Canadian Horse of the Year in 1970) in the USA in 1977. The latter two were found alive.

20TH-CENTURY RACECOURSE CLOSURES

On 31 December 1999, there were 59 racecourses in Britain. By coincidence, 59 other courses had closed in the previous 100 years:

Racecourse	*Last meeting*
Aldershot Military	1/4/1939
Alexandra Park	8/9/1970
Beaufort	14/4/1956
Birmingham	21/6/1965
Blackpool (Clifton Park)	26/4/1915
Bogside	10/4/1965
Bournemouth	10/4/1928
Bridgnorth	20/5/1939
Bridgwater	13/5/1904
Buckfastleigh	27/8/1960
Bungay	29/5/1939
Burgh-by-Sands	16/4/1900
Cardiff	27/4/1939
Carmarthen	17/4/1914
Chelmsford	29/4/1935
Colchester	4/4/1904
Colwall Park	25/5/1939
Cottenham	7/5/1925
Cowbridge	4/5/1939
Croxton Park	2/4/1914
Dawlish	20/9/1900
Derby	9/8/1939
Dunbar	22/3/1906
Gatwick	15/6/1940
Harpenden	7/5/1914
Hawthorn Hill	4/4/1939
Hethersett	4/5/1939
Hooton Park	26/12/1914
Hull	11/9/1909
Hurst Park	10/10/1962
Keele Park	12/5/1906

Racecourse	*Last meeting*
Lanark	18/10/1977
Lewes	14/9/1964
Lincoln	21/5/1964
Maiden Erlegh	12/4/1906
Maldon	29/4/1903
Malton	4/2/1904
Manchester	9/11/1963
Monmouth	4/5/1933
Newmarket Chases	28/12/1905
Newport	17/5/1948
Northampton	31/3/1904
Oswestry	29/4/1939
Paisley	10/8/1906
Pershore	1/5/1939
Picton	11/4/1914
Plymouth	5/9/1929
Portsmouth Park	13/4/1914
Ross-on-Wye	18/4/1904
Rothbury	10/4/1965
Sheffield	5/11/1901
Shincliffe	6/5/1914
Shirley Park	11/3/1940
Stockton	16/6/1981
Tarporley	26/4/1939
Tenby	29/10/1936
Torquay	25/3/1940
Totnes	1/9/1938
Wenlock	5/5/1939
Woore	1/6/1963
Wye	2/5/1974

A SUNDAY STROLL

In 1995 Harayir, ridden by Richard Hills trained by Major Dick Hern and owned by Hamdan Al Maktoum, won the 1000 Guineas. It was the first Classic to be held on a Sunday.

RACE CARDS INTRODUCED

The 1827 Derby was the first time racegoers enjoyed the privilege of reading a racecard. William Dorling produced the racecard for the Derby meeting at Epsom Downs complete with runners, riders, colours and pre-race odds.

GRAND NATIONAL'S FIRST LADY JOCKEY

In 1977 Miss Charlotte Brew became the first ever female jockey to ride in the Aintree Grand National. Up until 1977 women were not allowed to ride in the race but in 1976 Equal Opportunities legislation was introduced meaning that there was to be no discrimination in employment, which included jockeys participating in the Grand National. Brew's mount for the National, Barony Fort, qualified to run in the race after finishing fourth (last) in the Foxhunters. Barony Fort fell at the last open ditch (the fourth fence in the race).

CROSS-ATLANTIC CHALLENGE

In 1993 American jockey Gary Stevens became the youngest jockey (aged 30) to surpass $100 million in earnings. In 1999 he crossed the Atlantic to commence a new challenge as stable jockey to Sir Michael Stoute. The 36-year-old had ridden more than 4,500 winners in the USA before moving to Britain. His first challenge in England was the 1999 Epsom Derby, when he partnered Beat All, but it was not a dream start for Stevens, finishing third behind Kieren Fallon on Oath.

Gary Stevens was chosen and somehow found time to play the jockey George Woolf in the 2003 movie *Seabiscuit*. When he announced his retirement on 27 November 2005, he had won three Kentucky Derbies, three Belmont Stakes, two Preakness Stakes and the Santa Anita Derby a record nine times. He had also accumulated eight Breeders' Cup race victories. In total, Stevens won $221 million with 4,888 winners. An astonishing achievement given that Stevens spent 19 months in a leg brace as a child as a result of a degenerative disease to his hip.

SUBZERO CHAMPION

As part of his rehabilitation after injuring himself, and in order to be fit to ride at the 2008 Cheltenham Festival, Tony McCoy underwent sessions in a cryotherapy chamber at subzero temperatures.

DONKEY DERBY

Of the 26 runners in the 1962 Derby only 19 managed to finish the race following a major collision at a crowded Tattenham Corner. The accident led to six jockeys needing medical treatment, two of them suffering from concussion, while one horse had to be put down after breaking a leg. The accident occurred as a direct result of some horses falling back as others moved up the field, added to jockeys switching positions approaching Tattenham Corner. A stewards' enquiry after the race did not find anyone in particular to be responsible for the pile-up, but they did state that they were of the opinion that there were too many horses in the field that were simply not good enough. Larkspur, ridden by Neville Sellwood, trained by Vincent O'Brien and owned by Raymond Guest, won the Classic.

RACING JARGON (36)

Stewards' enquiry – the race stewards have the power to disqualify horses and revise the official result of a race if they are of the opinion that a jockey has broken any of the rules of racing during a race. An announcement is made after a race to let racegoers know that a stewards' enquiry has been called. Until the result of their deliberations is made known bookmakers are not permitted to settle bets.

SCOTLAND'S HERO

In 1979 Rubstic, ridden by Maurice Barnes, became the first Scottish-trained winner of the Aintree Grand National. His trainer John Leadbetter's yard was based in Roxburghshire.

WEBSITE FAVOURITES

Denman and his stablemate Kauto Star have their own fan clubs and boast their own sites on the website Facebook, with each horse claiming hundreds of cyber friends daily.

AN UNUSUAL US TRIPLE CROWN

In 1995 trainer D. Wayne Lukas landed the US Triple Crown with two different horses. Thunder Gulch won the Kentucky Derby and the Belmont Classic Stakes (ridden by Gary Stevens and owned by Michael Tabor), while Timber Country (ridden by Pat Day and owned by Overbrook/Gainesway/Lewis) claimed the Preakness Stakes.

INDEX

O